# HOW TO MAKE PERFECT
# PASTRY

# HOW TO MAKE PERFECT
# PASTRY

The fine art of pastry-making made easy with more than 75 tempting
step-by-step recipes shown in over 400 stunning photographs

**CATHERINE ATKINSON**

southwater

This edition is published by Southwater, an imprint of Anness Publishing Ltd,
Blaby Road, Wigston, Leicestershire LE18 4SE; info@anness.com

www.southwaterbooks.com; www.annesspublishing.com

If you like the images in this book and would like to investigate using them for publishing, promotions or advertising,
please visit our website www.practicalpictures.com for more information.

Publisher: Joanna Lorenz
Managing Editor: Linda Fraser
Editor: Joy Wotton
Additional Recipes: Alex Barker, Angela Boggiano, Carla Capalbo, Jacqueline Clarke, Carole Clements, Trish Davies, Roz Denny,
Matthew Drennan, Joanna Farrow, Christine France, Sarah Gates, Brian Glover, Nicola Graimes, Christine Ingram, Lucy Knox,
Norma MacMillan, Sue Maggs, Sally Mansfield, Maggie Mayhew, Norma Miller, Sallie Morris, Keith Richmond, Liz Trigg,
Hilaire Walden, Laura Washburn, Steven Wheeler and Elizabeth Wolf-Cohen
Props Stylist: Helen Trent
Special Photography: Janine Hosegood
Designers: Nigel Partridge and Isobel Gillan
Production Controller: Pirong Wang

© Anness Publishing Ltd 2012

Previously published as *Perfect Pastry*

NOTES
Bracketed terms are intended for American readers.
For all recipes, quantities are given in both metric and imperial measures and,
where appropriate, in standard cups and spoons.
Follow one set of measures, but not a mixture, because they are not interchangeable.
Standard spoon and cup measures are level. 1 tsp = 5ml, 1 tbsp = 15ml, 1 cup = 250ml/8fl oz.
Australian standard tablespoons are 20ml. Australian readers should use 3 tsp in place of 1 tbsp for measuring small quantities.
American pints are 16fl oz/2 cups. American readers should use 20fl oz/2.5 cups in place of 1 pint when measuring liquids.
Electric oven temperatures in this book are for conventional ovens. When using a fan oven, the temperature
will probably need to be reduced by about 10–20°C/20–40°F. Since ovens vary, you should check
with your manufacturer's instruction book for guidance.
Medium (US large) eggs are used unless otherwise stated.

Main front cover image shows Baked Cheesecake with Kissel – for recipe, see pages 116–17.

# CONTENTS

# THE ART OF PERFECT PASTRY

Nothing compares with the moment when an exquisitely prepared pastry dish arrives at the meal table. Whether a deep double-crust pie with gloriously golden crisp pastry, whose filling is yet to be revealed, a tartlet of fragile filo encasing smoked chicken with peach mayonnaise, or a sumptuous gâteau Saint-Honoré with a base of light puff pastry topped with caramel-coated puffs, such pastries are always greeted with cries of pleasure, and the tasting eagerly anticipated.

Few people can resist the tantalizing display of patisserie in a good quality bakers' window, but the fillings and flavour of shop-bought pastries sometimes fail to live up to expectation. While appearance is vital to tempt the eye, the palette should be equally enchanted and never disappointed. It's important to ensure that the pastry used is appropriate for the chosen filling and that both the flavours and textures work well together – robust hot-water crust pastry for example is the perfect partner for a rich and flavoursome game mixture, whereas a buttery biscuit-like pâte sucrée makes an excellent container for a smooth and creamy vanilla-scented custard filling.

Just as eating good pastry is immensely enjoyable, making your own can be equally satisfying. If you love to

*Above: A fresh-tasting exotic fruit tranche never fails to please.*

cook, perfecting melt-in-the mouth pastry and making professional-looking delicacies, is to discover an art that is not only full of traditional recipes, but also of creative possibilities. Pastry can be wonderfully varied. You can try using different flours and fats, changing their proportion to each other or combining them in different ways and perhaps adding flavourings or extra textural ingredients, to conjure up an infinite range that will complement sweet and savoury fillings. This enables you to make and bake all types of pastries from luxurious first courses to whet the appetite to pastry desserts that leave your guests happily replete.

Easy travel and communication has increased our knowledge of pastries from around the world and modern cooks are just as likely to bake an apple pie with filo pastry, as they are to use shortcrust or puff pastry. Ingredients that were once considered unusual or somewhat exotic are now widely available and the potential combinations of pastry and filling are limited only by the cook's imagination.

A superb and comprehensive collection of step-by-step pastries can be found here, including many well-loved classics as well as new and contemporary ideas. Many are delightfully simple and relatively quick to make such as peach and redcurrant tartlets or one-crust

rhubarb pie, while others are sumptuous indeed, for example, classic lemon meringue pie, filled with a rich lemon cream filling and heaped with golden-topped meringue.

To help you to perfect the art of pastry-making, a detailed reference section explains essential techniques, from baking basics to lining flan tins (quiche pans) and creating lattice top pies and intricate pastry decorations. Precise instructions for making pastry are given in individual recipes. Whatever the time of year or the occasion, this book will provide a wealth of recipes and ideas to suit your needs and to help you to discover the pleasure to be had from making pastry.

*Below: Chicken charter pie is a traditional recipe with timeless appeal.*

*Below: Gâteau Saint-Honoré always makes an eye-catching dessert.*

# PASTRY ESSENTIALS

Making pastry is based on a few golden rules, which, if adhered to, will ensure success every time. First, always measure ingredients accurately – even professionals with years of experience rely on weighing scales or calibrated measuring cups. Secondly, make sure you keep everything cool; the work surface, ingredients, utensils, your hands and even your temper, as pastry needs careful, light handling (although this rule does not apply to choux or hot-water crust pastry). Lastly, most pastries need to be rested and chilled after every stage of making and assembling. Don't cut down on the times suggested for this process, or your pastry may suffer.

*Right: Tins come in a range of sizes and shapes. They may have loose bases or clipped sides for easy removal of the pie or tart.*

## PASTRY INGREDIENTS

Good quality ingredients are at the heart of successful pastry-making, as only a few are needed. For traditional crisp pastries, plain (all-purpose) flour is best, although self-raising (self-rising) may be used for pastries such as suet crust. Pastry may be made with one fat, or a mixture of several. Butter on its own gives a rich flavour and wonderful colour and is absolutely essential for some such as puff pastry. Others, such as shortcrust, may be made with all butter or, for a shorter (crumblier) texture, a more traditional blend of

butter and white vegetable fat or lard. If margarine is preferred, use the hard block variety rather than soft-tub margarine. Sugar is added to pastries such as pâte sucrée to produce crisper baked results, but it is essential to watch the pastry during cooking as it colours more quickly.

## PASTRY EQUIPMENT

Using the right baking equipment simplifies and enhances the art of pastry-making. As your skills develop and you make more elaborate dishes, you may decide to invest in some of the vast wealth of specialist dishes, tins (pans), moulds and cutters available.

**Pie dishes** These have sloping sides and a wide flat rim. The traditional glazed earthenware ones are perfect for single-crust pies, but choose a metal dish when making double-crust pies and cook on a pre-heated heavy baking sheet to keep the pastry base crisp.

**Springform tins** Also known as spring-clip tins, these are round and straight-sided with a removable base and a clip on the side to release the pie.

*Left, clockwise from top left: Essential pastry ingredients include water, flour, butter, salt, eggs, sugar and lard.*

**Raised pie moulds** Designed to produce flawless, prettily decorated raised meat and game pies, these are hinged on one side to simplify the removal of the pie.

**Flan tins** Also known as quiche pans, these metal tins come in all shapes and sizes including square, rectangular, heart and petal-shaped, but the easiest to obtain is the fluted round. Loose-based tins are preferable as they make the turning out of fragile tarts simple.

**Flan rings** These come without bases and are designed to be set directly on a baking sheet. Choose a heavy baking sheet that won't warp when heated.

**Tranche tins** From the French, meaning slice, these long rectangular fluted tins make for easy serving as the finished flan can be simply cut across in slices.

**Porcelain flan dishes** Although their unglazed bases mean that the heat can penetrate, these dishes absorb heat much more slowly than metal ones, so they are not ideal for baking pastry but are best used as a serving dish.

**Tartlet tins** These come in a multitude of shapes and sizes. Round ones for individual tartlets are popular, as are boat-shaped moulds, known as bâteau and barquette moulds.

**Cornet moulds** These metal cones, just over 10cm/4in long, are used to shape pastry horns. Strips of pastry are wound around them, then baked.

**Cannoli forms** Similar to cornet moulds, these tubes are open at both ends.

# MAKING PASTRY

There is no need to feel apprehensive when working with pastry, even if it's your first time. The dos and don'ts are well known and there is no better – or more enjoyable – way to learn than by making your own.

This section contains recipes for classic shortcrust pastry and its enriched variations, as well as for the traditional suet, puff, choux and hot water crust pastries. There are also variations with a tasty twist: cheese pastry and fresh herb pastry.

## SHORTCRUST PASTRY

This short, crumbly pastry is probably the best known and most frequently used type. Although the simplest of all pastries, perfect shortcrust needs a cool light hand, as over-handling the dough will develop the gluten in the flour, making it heavy and hard. The following makes enough for a 25cm/10in flan tin (quiche pan) or ten 7.5cm/3in tartlet tins (mini quiche pans).

MAKES ABOUT 375G/13OZ

INGREDIENTS
   225g/8oz/2 cups plain
    (all-purpose) flour
   pinch of salt
   115g/4oz/½ cup chilled butter,
    diced, or half butter and half lard
    or white vegetable fat
   45–60ml/3–4 tbsp chilled water

**1** Sift the flour and salt together into a mixing bowl. Cut the fat into the flour using a pastry blender or use your fingertips to rub it in. Shake the bowl occasionally to bring any large pieces of fat to the top. Blend until the mixture resembles fine breadcrumbs.

**2** Sprinkle 45ml/3 tbsp of the water evenly over the mixture and mix lightly with a round-bladed knife or fork until the dough comes together. Add a little more water if the mixture is still too dry; it should just begin to hold together.

**3** Using one hand, gather the dough together to form a ball. Incorporate any loose pieces of the rubbed-in mixture. Knead on a lightly floured surface for just a few seconds until smooth.

**4** Wrap the dough in clear film (plastic wrap), and chill for about 30 minutes, or until firm but not too stiff to roll. The shortcrust pastry is now ready to use.

> **Variations**
> Once you've mastered making shortcrust, try adding flavourings to vary the rubbed-in mixture.
> **Cheese pastry** Add 50g/2oz/½ cup grated mature Cheddar or 45ml/3 tbsp freshly grated Parmesan and a pinch of mustard powder.
> **Fresh herb pastry** Add 45ml/3 tbsp chopped fresh herbs such as parsley, sage or chives or 15ml/1 tbsp stronger flavoured herbs such as rosemary or thyme.

## RICH SHORTCRUST PASTRY

Also known as pâte brisée, this is a richer version of shortcrust pastry with a higher proportion of fat. It is usually made with an egg yolk and chilled water, but a whole egg may be used. This quantity is enough for a 25cm/10in flan tin (quiche pan) or ten 7.5cm/3in tartlet tins (mini quiche pans).

MAKES ABOUT 400G/14OZ

INGREDIENTS
   225g/8oz/2 cups plain
    (all-purpose) flour
   pinch of salt
   150g/5oz/10 tbsp chilled butter,
    diced
   1 egg yolk
   30ml/2 tbsp chilled water

**1** Sift the flour and salt into a large bowl. Rub or cut in the butter until the mixture resembles fine breadcrumbs.

**2** Mix the egg yolk and water together. Sprinkle over the dry ingredients and mix in lightly to form a soft dough.

**3** Gather the dough together into a ball. Knead on a floured surface until smooth. Wrap in clear film (plastic wrap) and chill for 30 minutes before using.

## MAKING SHORTCRUST PASTRY IN A FOOD PROCESSOR

This method of making pastry is good for rich shortcrust, especially where the higher proportion of fat and sugar may make it harder to handle. If you have hot hands, or the weather is warm, the food processor ensures that the dough stays cool.

**1** Put the sifted flour, salt and sugar, if using, into the food processor. Process for 4–5 seconds. Scatter the cubes of fat over the dry ingredients. Process for 10–12 seconds only, or until the mixture resembles fine breadcrumbs.

**2** Sprinkle the water or other liquid (such as egg and water) over the flour mixture and, using the pulse button, process until it starts to hold together. Pinch a little of the mixture between your finger and thumb; if the dough is too dry and crumbly, add a little more water and process for just 1–2 seconds more. Do not allow the pastry to form a ball in the food processor.

**3** Remove the mixture and form into a ball. Lightly knead on a floured surface for just a few seconds until smooth, then wrap in clear film (plastic wrap) and chill for 30 minutes.

## PATE SUCREE

This rich and crisp-textured sweet pastry, also known as biscuit pastry, is used mainly for making flan and tartlet cases, as it holds its shape well during cooking. Because pâte sucrée has a high proportion of sugar, it is a much softer pastry than shortcrust and needs to be chilled for 1 hour before using. It is made with icing (confectioners') sugar, but caster sugar may be used. As with French flan pastry, it is lightly kneaded by a process known as *fresage* using the heel of the hand. Mix the pastry either in a bowl or – the classic way – on a marble slab or other cold surface. This quantity is enough for a 23cm/9in flan tin (quiche pan) or eight 7.5cm/3in tartlet tins (mini quiche pans).

MAKES ABOUT 275G/10OZ

INGREDIENTS
  150g/5oz/1¼ cups plain
    (all-purpose) flour
  pinch of salt
  75g/3oz/6 tbsp chilled butter, diced
  25g/1oz/¼ cup icing (confectioners')
    sugar, sifted
  2 egg yolks

**1** Sift the flour and salt together to make a mound on a marble slab, pastry board or cold work surface. Make a well in the centre and put in the butter and sugar, then place the egg yolks on top.

**2** Using your fingertips only, and using a pecking action, work the butter, yolks and sugar together until the mixture resembles scrambled eggs. As you do this, pull in a little of the surrounding flour to prevent the mixture from becoming too sticky.

**3** When the mixture begins to form a smooth paste, pull in more of the flour to make a rough dough, gradually working in all the flour. Work quickly, using just your fingertips, so that the butter does not become oily. If the pastry is slightly crumbly at this stage, you can remedy this by working a small amount of egg white into the dough.

**4** Lightly knead the dough with just the heel of your hand for about 1 minute, pushing small portions of dough away from you and smearing them on the surface until smooth and pliable.

**5** Shape the dough into a ball, then flatten slightly into a flat round – this makes it easier when you start rolling it out. Wrap in clear film (plastic wrap) to prevent the pastry from drying out and chill for about 1 hour before using.

## SUET PASTRY

This pastry can be used for both sweet and savoury steamed puddings and has a light, spongy texture. It is wonderfully easy to make as there is no rubbing-in. Because suet is a heavy fat, self-raising flour is always used for this recipe. Lower-fat or vegetarian suet may also be used. This quantity is sufficient to line a 1.75 litre/3 pint/7½ cup ovenproof bowl.

MAKES ABOUT 500G/1¼LB

INGREDIENTS
275g/10oz/2½ cups self-raising
   (self-rising) flour
2.5ml/½ tsp salt
150g/5oz/1 cup shredded suet
175ml/6fl oz/¾ cup chilled water

**1** Sift the flour and salt into a large mixing bowl.

**2** Stir in the shredded suet, followed by most of the chilled water (you may need a little less or more) and mix with a fork or spoon to form a soft dough.

**3** Knead on a lightly floured surface for a few seconds until smooth. Roll out the suet pastry and use straight away. Don't be tempted to roll the pastry too thinly. It needs to be about 1cm/½in thick.

## PUFF PASTRY

Light and crisp, with a distinctly buttery flavour, puff pastry (pâte feuilletée) is the richest, yet lightest, of all pastries. It contains an equal amount of butter to flour. Air is trapped between the layers of dough and this, together with the steam created as the water heats, makes the pastry rise up when baked.

Although you need to allow plenty of time, puff pastry does not require continuous work; just a few minutes of re-rolling about every half hour.

It is essential that everything be kept cold when you are making puff pastry. The water should be chilled and the butter cold, but not so cold that it will break up and tear the dough; before commencing let the butter stand at room temperature for 10 minutes. Never make puff pastry on a hot day. This makes enough for two single-crusts in 1.5 litre/2½ pint/6¼ cup pie dishes or fifteen 8.5cm/3½in vol-au-vents.

MAKES ABOUT 500G/1¼LB

INGREDIENTS
225g/8oz/2 cups strong white
   bread flour
pinch of salt
225g/8oz/1 cup chilled butter
15ml/1 tbsp lemon juice
150ml/¼ pint/⅔ cup chilled water

**1** Sift the flour and salt into a mixing bowl. Rub or cut in 25g/1oz/2 tbsp of the butter into the flour until the mixture resembles fine breadcrumbs.

**2** Place the remaining butter between two sheets of clear film (plastic wrap) and gently beat it out into a 15cm/6in flat square with a rolling pin.

**3** Make a well in the centre of the dry ingredients. Stir the lemon juice into the water and add most of it to the bowl. Mix together with a round-bladed knife, adding a little more water if necessary to make a soft, but not sticky, dough.

**4** Using a floured rolling pin, roll out the dough on a lightly floured surface to a 25cm/10in square. The dough may look a little lumpy at this stage, but don't knead it. Place the butter diagonally in the centre of the dough, so that it looks like a diamond. Bring each corner of the dough to the centre of the butter to enclose it completely.

**5** Roll out the dough to a 40 × 15cm/ 16 × 6in rectangle, then fold the lower third of the pastry over the centre third, and the top third of the pastry down over that. Seal the edges by pressing down with the rolling pin. Brush off any excess flour with a dry pastry brush, then wrap the pastry in clear film and chill for 30 minutes.

**6** Roll out the pastry to the same size again, with the sealed edges at the top and bottom. Fold up and chill as before. Repeat the rolling, folding and chilling process five more times. After this, the pastry is ready to be used.

## CHOUX PASTRY

Elegantly light and crisp, choux pastry puffs up during baking to at least double its original size, creating a hollow centre, perfect for both sweet and savoury fillings.

Choux is one of the easiest pastries to make; follow the instructions and you can't go wrong. Unlike other pastries, where the fat is rubbed into the flour, choux is made on the hob (stovetop). The butter is melted with water then brought to the boil before adding the flour. Beating the mixture over a low heat partially cooks the flour. Finally, eggs are gradually incorporated to make a thick glossy paste, ready for spooning or piping into puffs and éclairs, or for making an impressive gâteaux such as Paris-Brest and Gâteau Saint-Honoré. This quantity is sufficient for 20 small puffs, 14 large puffs or 12 éclairs.

MAKES ABOUT 150G/5OZ

INGREDIENTS
  65g/2½oz/9 tbsp plain
    (all-purpose) flour
  pinch of salt
  50g/2oz/¼ cup butter, diced
  150ml/¼ pint/⅔ cup water
  2 eggs, lightly beaten

**1** Preheat the oven to 200°C/400°F/ Gas 6. Sift the flour and salt on to a small sheet of baking parchment. Put the butter and water in a pan and heat very gently until the butter has melted.

**2** Increase the heat and bring to a rolling boil. Remove the pan from the heat and immediately tip in all the flour and beat vigorously until the flour is mixed into the liquid.

**3** Return the pan to a low heat and beat the mixture until it begins to form a ball and leave the sides of the pan. This will take about 1 minute. Remove the pan from the heat again and allow to cool for 2–3 minutes.

**4** Add the beaten eggs a little at a time, beating well between each addition, until you have a very smooth shiny paste, thick enough to hold its shape. (You may not have to add all the egg.)

**5** Spoon or pipe the pastry on to a baking sheet dampened or lined with baking parchment. Space well apart.

### VARIATIONS
For a savoury choux pastry, sift up to 2.5ml/½ tsp mustard powder with the flour. Alternatively, add 75g/3oz/¾ cup grated mature Cheddar or Parmesan.

## HOT WATER CRUST PASTRY

This traditional British pastry is used for cold meat and game pies as it holds its shape and can withstand long cooking. The use of boiling water causes the fat to melt and results in a pastry that is strong whether it is uncooked or cooked. Hot water crust pies are known as standing or raised pies because they can hold their shape and stand unsupported by a tin or dish.

The following recipe makes enough pastry for a 20cm/8in raised pie mould or loose-based cake tin or a 25 x 7.5cm/ 10 x 3in oblong raised pie mould. Use the dough while it is still warm, since as the lard starts to set the pastry will become unmanageable and may crack.

MAKES ABOUT 450G/1LB

INGREDIENTS
  275g/10oz/2½ cups plain
    (all-purpose) flour
  1.5ml/¼ tsp salt
  65g/2½oz/5 tbsp lard or white
    vegetable fat
  150ml/¼ pint/⅔ cup water

**1** Sift the flour and salt into a bowl and make a well in the centre.

**2** Gently heat the fat and water in a pan until the fat has melted. Increase the heat and bring to the boil. Pour the hot liquid into the dry ingredients and mix to a soft dough.

**3** Knead in the bowl for a few seconds until smooth. Wrap the dough in clear film (plastic wrap) and leave to rest in a warm place for 10 minutes, or until the dough feels firmer and is cool enough to handle. Use while still warm.

# MAKING FLANS AND PIES

When you are nearly ready to roll and line or cut and layer your chosen pastry into flans, pies or tartlets, remove it from the refrigerator and let it stand at room temperature for 15 minutes so that it can soften slightly.

## LINING FLAN AND TARTLET TINS

**1** On a lightly floured surface, roll out the pastry until it is 5–7.5cm/2–3in larger all round than the tin (pan), depending on its depth. Fold the edge of the pastry over the rolling pin, then roll the pastry loosely around the pin. Lift the pastry over the tin.

**2** Gently press the pastry over the base and against the sides of the tin. Turn any surplus pastry outwards over the edge, then roll the rolling pin over the top of the tin to cut off the excess dough. Prick the base all over with a fork, to stop it rising up during baking.

**Tartlet tins** When lining tartlet tins (mini quiche pans) of less than 5cm/2in in diameter, place them close together, then roll out the pastry until it is about 3mm/⅛in thick and able to cover all the tins. Lift the pastry and drape it over. Using a floured thumb, gently press the pastry into the tins. Roll over the top with a rolling pin to trim off any excess.

## LINING PIE DISHES

There are three different ways to make a pie. The first is to line it in the same way as lining a tart tin and then fill it; the second is to have a single piece of pastry covering the pie filling (single-crust) and the third is to enclose the filling between two layers of pastry (double-crust). When using plain, rich shortcrust or puff pastry roll it to 3mm/⅛in thick. Puff pastry is best used only for single-crust pies.

**Single-crust pies** Roll out the pastry so that it is slightly larger than the pie dish and cut off a 2.5cm/1in strip around the edge. Moisten the rim of the pie dish, position the strip on the rim and brush with water. Add the filling, then cover with the pastry. After trimming, "knock up" the pastry edge by holding the blunt edge of a knife horizontally against the rim and tapping sharply.

**Double-crust pies** Roll out half of the pastry to 5cm/2in larger than the pie dish. Lift it into the dish. Fill the pastry case making a domed shape. Brush the edges of the pastry with water, then roll out the rest of the pastry slightly larger than the pie and place on top. Seal the edges together and trim the excess pastry with a knife. Knock up the pastry edges.

## MAKING FILO PASTRY PIES

Extremely easy to use, filo comes stacked into sheets, factory-rolled to a thinness that only a pastry chef could achieve. Keep the stack covered with a slightly damp dishtowel and peel off only the sheet that you're working with. It can be used to make all manner of pies from filled pastry cases to incredibly simple one-crust and scrunch toppings. Brush sparingly between the layers with cooled melted butter or oil, so that the baked pastry is crisp, and avoid very moist fillings, or the steam may spoil the texture of the filo.

**Lining a tin with filo** Brush a sheet of filo pastry with butter or oil, then use to line the base and sides of the tin. Brush a second sheet of pastry as before, then place on top of the first sheet. Layer the pastry to the desired thickness; four or five sheets are usually enough. Neaten the edges by trimming with a pair of scissors. If the sheets of filo aren't large enough to completely cover a tin, such as a tranche tin, use two sheets for each layer and overlap a little in the middle.

**One-crust filo topping** Take five to six sheets of filo pastry and cut them so that they are slightly larger than your chosen pie dish. Spoon the filling into the dish and top with the sheets of filo, lightly buttering or oiling between the layers. Tuck the filo edges down the sides of the dish to fit smoothly.

**Scrunch topping** Loosely crumple sheets of buttered or oiled filo and place fat-side up to cover the filling. Don't pack them too closely, or the cooked filo may have a doughy texture.

## CREATING DECORATIVE EDGES

The edges of flans and pies can be given a final flourish by decorating in a number of attractive ways. This can be as simple as making a pattern with the back of a fork to crimping and braiding. For some patterns, the pastry will be naturally thick enough around the edge – this is usually the case with puff pastry – but shortcrust and its variations may need a double thickness.

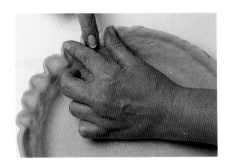

**Ruffled edges** Trim the pastry to leave an overhang of about 1cm/½in all round and fold under. Place the thumb and forefinger inside the pastry's edge and use the forefinger of the other hand to push the dough between them, to create a scalloped edge. Continue all round.

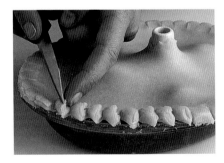

**Zig-zag edges** Make small cuts in the pastry edge about 1cm/½in apart all the way around. Brush with water, then fold each section over on to itself to form a small triangle. Use on dishes with a rim wider than 1cm/½in.

**Gabled edges** Trim the pastry even with the rim of the dish. Use a knife to make an even number of cuts about 1cm/½in apart all the way around. Fold alternate pieces of pastry inwards. Use on dishes with a rim of more than 1cm/½in.

## DECORATING A PIE WITH A LATTICE TOP

**1** Cut strips of pastry 1cm/½in wide using a knife or a fluted pastry wheel and a ruler. Lay half the strips across the pie, keeping them evenly spaced and parallel. Fold back to the centre every other strip. Lay another strip across the centre on the flat strips, at right angles to them. Lay the folded strips flat again.

**2** Fold back those strips that were not folded the first time. Lay another strip across those now flat. Continue folding the strips in this way until half of the lattice is completed. Repeat on the other half of the pie.

**3** Trim the ends of the strips even with the rim of the pie dish. Moisten the edge of the pastry case with water and seal. Decorate the edge as you like.

## MAKING PASTRY DECORATIONS

**Making tassels** These often decorate meat and game pies. Cut a long rectangle of pastry 15 × 2.5cm/6 × 1in. Make 2cm/¾in long cuts, at intervals of 5mm/¼in. Brush a little egg on the uncut portion of one end, then roll up tightly. Open out the tassels.

**Making leaves** A leaf-shaped cutter may be used, or cut rolled-out pastry into strips about 2.5cm/1in wide, then cut these diagonally into diamonds. Use the back of a knife to mark veins and pinch each leaf at one end to form a stalk.

**Making shells** Ideal for pies with a fish or seafood filling. Cut a strip of pastry 10 × 1cm/4 × ½in and wrap it round the pointed end of a cornet mould. Trim the end to a curve and press to seal. Bake the shells on the moulds.

# BAKING PASTRY

Whatever type of pastry you are baking, always allow time to preheat the oven; it will take about 15 minutes to reach the required temperature (fan ovens may heat more quickly). As a general rule, bake pastry on the middle shelf or just above the middle of the oven, unless the recipe tells you otherwise. If you are blind-baking or cooking a double-crust pie, it's a good idea to put a heavy baking sheet in the oven to heat up. The hot baking sheet will give the base of the pie an initial blast of heat to help ensure the bottom of the pastry is crisp. It will also make it easier to slide the pie in and out of the oven.

When following a recipe, baking times may vary slightly depending on your oven and how chilled the pie was when cooking commenced. Always check the pie at least 5 minutes before the end of the suggested cooking time. Don't keep opening the oven door though, or the temperature will drop, the pastry will be less crisp and it will inevitably take longer to cook.

## BAKING SHORTCRUST PASTRY

Shortcrust pastry and its variations should be well chilled before baking to mimimize shrinkage. Between 30–60 minutes is adequate for a flan or pie that is filled prior to baking; left much longer, the filling may start to soak into the pastry. If a flan case is to be blind-baked or filled just before baking, chill the pastry for an hour uncovered, or cover with clear film (plastic wrap) and chill overnight.

Shortcrust-type pastries are usually baked at 200°C/400°F/Gas 6, but often the temperature is reduced part-way through baking to allow the filling time to cook sufficiently. Take care with any pastries that contain added sugar; such pastries need to be removed from the oven as soon as the pastry has become golden brown because once this stage is reached, they can burn very quickly.

Don't cook any foods that will release a lot of steam in the oven at the same time as the shortcrust is cooking since this could prevent the pastry from becoming crisp.

## BAKING BLIND

This process is used for a number of reasons. Sometimes it is used to cook an empty pastry case so that the pastry does not become soggy when the filling is added to the case and the final baking is done. Baking blind may be used to bake a pastry case completely when the chosen filling cooks in a relatively short time. It is also used when the pastry case is to contain a precooked mixture or one that does not require any cooking at all.

**1** Cut out a round of baking parchment or foil about 7.5cm/3in larger than the flan tin (quiche pan). Prick the base of the pastry case all over with a fork.

**2** Place a round of baking parchment or foil about 7.5cm/3in larger than the flan tin (quiche pan) in the pastry case. Put either commercially made ceramic baking beans, or dried beans in the case in an even layer.

**3** To partially bake the pastry, bake in a preheated oven at 200°C/400°F/Gas 6 for 10 minutes, or until the pastry is set and the rim is dry and golden. Lift out the paper and beans. Return the case to the oven for a further 5 minutes.

**4** To fully bake the pastry, bake at 200°C/400°F/Gas 6 for 15 minutes, then remove the paper and beans and return to the oven. Bake for a further 5–10 minutes, or until golden brown. Cool completely before filling.

**5** To bake tartlets, bake blind in the same way as flans, but allow only 6–8 minutes for partial baking and 12–15 minutes for fully baked pastry.

### Shortcrust baking tips

• If you find any small holes in a cooked pastry case, repair them by brushing with a little beaten egg, then return the case to the oven for 2–3 minutes to seal. Any larger holes or tears that appear during baking should be repaired by pressing a little raw pastry in the gap; brush with beaten egg, and then return the case to the oven.
• If the pastry starts to bubble up during baking, remove the pastry case from the oven, prick again with a fork to allow the trapped air to escape and return to the oven. If it has bubbled up when you take it out after cooking, don't try to press it flat, or you will crack the pastry. Make a very small slit in the case with a knife and leave it to shrink back on its own.
• If the pastry has fully browned

before the filling is completely cooked, protect it by covering with foil. Cover single- or double-crust pies completely, making a hole in the top of the foil to allow steam to escape. On open flans, cover the pastry edge only with strips of foil.

## BAKING PUFF AND FLAKY PASTRY

The baking method for puff, rough puff and flaky pastry has much in common with that used for shortcrust. Chilling the pastry before baking is essential, and shaped puff pastries should be chilled for at least an hour to prevent the pastry becoming mis-shapen during baking. Take great care when brushing the pastry with egg glaze; any that runs down the sides of the pastry will make the layers stick together and prevent the pastry from rising well and evenly.

Layered pastries must be cooked in a preheated hot oven, so that the air trapped within the layers expands and, together with the steam produced by the water, lifts up the pastry. If the oven is too cool, the butter will melt before the dough has a chance to cook, preventing the pastry from rising well. The oven temperature is usually 230°C/450°F/Gas 8, but small pastries are sometimes cooked at 220°C/425°F/Gas 7. Reduce the temperature after about 15 minutes, to give the filling time to cook through.

When baking single- and double-crust pies, up to three (depending how moist the filling is) slits or holes should be made in the pastry top to allow the steam from the filling to escape. Don't make too many steam holes though, or too much air will be lost and the pastry won't rise well. After baking, cover steam holes with cooked pastry decorations.

Unlike shortcrust pastries, a steamy atmosphere helps puff pastry to rise. Put a dish of hot water on the lowest shelf when preheating the oven. Remove it for the last few minutes of cooking. If the pastry starts to sink after cooking, it hasn't cooked sufficiently and should be returned to the oven for a little longer.

## BAKING FILO PASTRY

Unlike shortcrust and puff pastries, filo pastry does not require chilling before baking. The most important point to remember is that filo must never dry out, or it will become brittle and hard to fold and shape. Keep the sheets you are not working with covered with a damp dishtowel. It may also crumble if it is too cold so, before using, remove the unopened packet from the refrigerator and allow to stand for 30 minutes.

Filo must always be lightly brushed with melted butter before baking to give it a shiny glaze – unsalted (sweet) butter is perfect because it has a lower water content, or oil can also be used. Choose a mild oil, such as groundnut (peanut) or sunflower oil, or try olive oil when making well-flavoured savoury pastries. Don't overdo the fat though; it should be brushed as thinly and evenly as possible to create light crisp layers. Never brush filo with egg or milk as this would make it soggy.

The usual temperature for baking filo pastry is 200°C/400°F/Gas 6, although it can be cooked at a slightly lower temperature without its crisp texture being affected. It colours quickly, so check frequently towards the end of the cooking time. If the pastry has browned sufficiently before the filling is cooked, cover it loosely with foil, then remove again for the last few minutes to make sure the top of the pie is dry and crisp.

Wrap any unused filo in clear film (plastic wrap) and return it to the refrigerator. It will keep for seven to ten days. It is possible to re-freeze filo, but don't do this more than once. To thaw, allow 4 hours at room temperature, or leave overnight in the refrigerator.

### Glazing pastry before baking

The appearance of almost every pie can be improved with a glaze. Even a simple brushing of milk or egg white will give the pastry case a lovely finish.

**Egg wash** Whole beaten egg can be used, or for a rich, glossy finish, lightly beat 1 egg yolk with 5ml/1 tsp cold water in a bowl, then beat in a pinch of salt or caster (superfine) sugar, depending on whether you are glazing a sweet or savoury pie. For a deeper coloured glaze, chill after the first glazing, then apply a second coat. Brush thinly, taking care the glaze doesn't pool around any decorative edges, or they will be much darker after baking.

**Saffron egg glaze** This gives pastry a vibrant, golden colour and is ideal for fish, seafood and chicken pies. Add a pinch of saffron threads to a small bowl containing 15ml/1 tbsp boiling water. Leave for 20 minutes, then strain into beaten egg or egg yolk.

**Egg white** Lightly beaten egg white gives a clear, shiny finish. On sweet pastries, sprinkle the egg white with caster (superfine) sugar.

**Milk** This is used when a very light glaze with little shine is needed. Use on sweet pies made with rich shortcrust pastry as these already have a good colour from the egg yolks in the pastry.

# SHAPING AND BAKING CHOUX PASTRY

This thick, smooth and glossy paste can be piped or spooned into a variety of shapes including round puffs, finger-lengths and rings. It can also be fried to make churros and French aigrettes, which are crunchy on the outside and soft in the centre. Choux is made on the hob (stovetop) and should be shaped while warm for the best results.

## PIPING CHOUX PASTRY

Before piping, you may find it helpful to draw faint guidelines on the baking parchment first, then place the paper pencil-side down on the baking sheet.
**Rounds** Use a piping bag fitted with a 1cm/½in plain or fluted nozzle to make small puffs and, for large puffs, use a 2.5cm/1in plain nozzle. Use a wet knife to cut off the pastry at the nozzle.

**Eclairs** Spoon the pastry into a piping bag fitted with a 2.5cm/1in plain nozzle. Pipe 10cm/4in lengths on to baking parchment, using a wet knife to cut off the pastry at the nozzle.

**Ring** Draw a 18cm/7in circle on baking parchment. Place pencil-side down on a baking sheet. Spoon the choux pastry into a piping bag fitted with a 1cm/½in nozzle and pipe a ring using the pencil marking as a guide.

## SHAPING CHOUX PUFFS

Whether spooned or piped, these balls of choux pastry will rise to about three times their original size, creating a hollow centre that is ready for filling. Make small ones into profiteroles with a cream filling and a chocolate sauce or pile into a pyramid held together with caramel for the classic French dessert croquembouche. Larger ones can be turned into cream buns.

**Small and large puffs** To make small puffs, use two small spoons dipped in water. Drop the paste in 2.5cm/1in wide balls on to a greased baking sheet, or one lined with baking parchment, leaving a 4cm/1½in space between each. For large puffs, use two large spoons to make balls 5cm/2in wide. Neaten the puffs with a spoon, dipped in water.

## FRYING PIPED CHOUX

Choux pastry can be deep-fried in hot oil rather than baked, giving a crisp, golden outside and a soft, light centre.

Spoon the choux into a piping bag fitted with a large star nozzle. Pipe four or five 7.5cm/3in lengths of pastry at a time into hot oil, using a pair of scissors to snip off each length. Fry for 3 minutes until crisp, then drain on kitchen paper.

## BAKING CHOUX

No matter what shape or size, choux pastry should be dark golden and crisp on the outside and cooked sufficiently so that it holds its shape when removed from the oven. For this reason, choux is usually baked at a higher temperature first, to cook the outside, then at a lower one to firm and dry the pastry.

Bake small puffs in a preheated oven at 200°C/400°F/Gas 6 for 15–20 minutes; large puffs, eclairs and rings will take 25–30 minutes. Turn down the oven to 180°C/350°F/Gas 4, remove the tray from the oven, make small slits in the sides of the pastries, then return and bake small puffs for a further 5 minutes; large puffs, eclairs and rings for a further 8–12 minutes.

It is important not to open the oven during the first 15 minutes of baking time or the choux may collapse. When you remove the pastries to make slits in them, check that they are fully cooked and set first.

The more steam in the oven at the start of baking, the more successfully the pastry will rise. Try dampening the baking sheet by sprinkling with cold water before spooning or piping the pastry, or place an ovenproof dish of water on the lowest shelf of the oven. Remove the dish for the last 5 minutes of cooking time to allow the pastries to become properly crisp.

Choux pastries are best freshly made, but will keep for a day or two in an airtight container. Put them on a baking sheet in a medium oven for 3–4 minutes to regain their crispness. Once filled, serve them as soon as possible, or they will become soggy.

# SHAPING AND BAKING HOT WATER CRUST

This pastry is used for traditional cold meat and game pies as it holds its shape and can withstand long cooking.

## MOULDING HOT WATER CRUST PASTRY

Keep this pastry warm while moulding; if the lard starts to set, the pastry will become unmanageable and may crack.

**1** Make a basic quantity of dough, and cut off one-third. Wrap it in clear film (plastic wrap) and leave in a warm place. Shape the remaining two-thirds of the pastry into a ball. Lightly grease and flour the outside of an empty 900g/2lb jam jar, turn it upside-down, mould the dough over the base and two-thirds down the sides.

**2** Cover with clear film and chill for 20 minutes, then invert the pastry case and jar on to a baking sheet and ease out the jam jar. Spoon the filling into the pastry mould, packing it firmly. Roll out the reserved pastry to a round and trim to fit the top of the pie.

**3** Wrap the trimmings and set aside. Dampen the edges and place the lid on top. Crimp the edges together neatly. Make a hole in the top of the pie with a 1cm/½in plain pastry cutter. Attach pastry trimmings, if you wish.

**4** Secure a double layer of baking parchment, cut to size, around the pie with paper clips to keep the pastry in shape during cooking.

## LINING A TIN WITH HOT WATER CRUST PASTRY

To line a 15cm/6in round cake tin, you need to use 350g/12oz/3 cups plain (all-purpose) flour, 1.5ml/¼ tsp of salt, 75g/3oz/6 tbsp fat and 190ml/6½fl oz/ generous ¾ cup warm water.

To line a 23cm/9in long pointed oval pie tin, or a 20cm/8in round springform tin, use the following: 450g/1lb/4 cups plain flour, 2.5ml/½ tsp salt, 115g/4oz/ ½ cup fat and 250ml/8fl oz/1 cup water.

**1** Make a basic quantity of dough. Cut off slightly less than a third, wrap in clear film (plastic wrap) and set aside in a warm place. Roll out the remaining pastry to a round large enough to line the tin. Carefully lift the pastry in, allowing the edges to hang over the sides. Gently press with your fingers to mould the pastry into place, then spoon in the filling, packing it down firmly.

**2** Trim off the overhanging pastry edges, angling the knife outwards. Wrap the pastry trimmings and set them aside for later use as decorations.

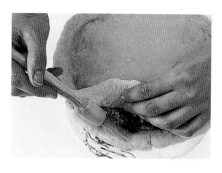

**3** Roll out the reserved pastry to make a lid slightly larger than the top of the tin. Brush the edges with water and place the lid over the pie. Gently press the edges together to seal, then lightly crimp the pastry to give it a fluted edge.

## BAKING HOT WATER CRUST PASTRY

As hot water crust pastry cooks the outside becomes crunchy and golden and the juices and fat from the pie filling seep into the pastry and flavour it.

Hot water crust pies are usually cooked at 200°C/400°F/Gas 6 for the first 20–30 minutes, then at a reduced temperature of 180°C/350°F/Gas 4 or lower for the remaining cooking time.

**1** Use a small cutter to make a steam hole, or cut a cross in the lid and fold back the corners. Make decorations with the reserved pastry trimmings and bake them separately, or place them on the crust to cook.

**2** After baking, put a funnel through the hole in the pastry lid and carefully pour in aspic jelly until it reaches the level of the pastry lid. Replace or add the cooked pastry decorations and then chill until the jelly has set. If the jelly starts to leak through a crack in the pastry, seal it by filling with butter.

# MAKING PARCELS AND CASES

Without the restrictions of flan tins (quiche pans) and pie dishes, there are an infinite number of ways to shape pastry packages and containers. Shortcrust and puff pastries and their variations, as well as filo can all be used in this way.

## SHAPING SHORTCRUST PASTRY

Rounds, strips, crescents and squares of shortcrust pastry provide the perfect package for sweet and savoury fillings.

### Making round parcels

**1** For sweet fillings of thinly sliced raw fruit such as apples and pears, or cooked and drained juicier fruits such as gooseberries, roll out 450g/1lb shortcrust pastry to a thickness of 3mm/⅛in and cut four 10cm/4in rounds and four slightly larger rounds, about 13cm/5in in diameter. Using a small, round cutter, stamp a small hole out of the middle of the larger rounds. Spoon a little filling in a rounded heap on the smaller rounds.

**2** Brush the edges of the filled pastry rounds with a little water, cover with the larger rounds of pastry and crimp the edges together. Bake the pastry rounds at 200°C/400°F/Gas 6 for 20 minutes.

### Making crescents

These are ideal for rich fruit or cream or curd cheese fillings and should be made with rich shortcrust pastry as it is flexible. Roll out 450g/1lb pastry to 3mm/⅛in thick and stamp out rounds using a plain or fluted 7.5cm/3in cutter. Place the filling on one side of each. Brush with milk, then fold over and seal. Make steam holes and bake at 200°C/400°F/Gas 6 for 18–20 minutes.

### Making pasties

In these traditional single-serving pies, the filling is usually a mixture of either raw or cooked minced (ground) meat and vegetables, but pre-cooked fillings such as apple work equally well. You can also cook pasties on their side or make turnovers by cutting the pastry into squares and folding into triangles.

**1** Roll out 450g/1lb shortcrust pastry to a thickness of 5mm/¼in and cut into four 20cm/8in rounds. Spoon the filling into the centre of each round and brush the edges with water. Bring the edges together to seal, then flute.

**2** Transfer to a baking sheet, brush with beaten egg and make a steam hole in the top of each one. For uncooked fillings, bake at 220°C/425°F/Gas 7 for 15 minutes, then at 160°C/325°F/Gas 3 and bake for 1 hour more. If using a pre-cooked filling, bake at 200°C/400°F/Gas 6 for 20–25 minutes.

### Making fruit dumplings

Whole peeled and cored fresh fruit is delicious wrapped in pastry and then baked. Use firm, fresh apples and pears.

**1** Roll out 400g/14oz rich shortcrust pastry to a 35cm/14in square and cut into four squares. Place a prepared fruit in the middle of each.

**2** Brush the edges with beaten egg and pull up the four corners to meet at the top, sealing well, then flute.

**3** Chill for 40 minutes, then glaze. Bake at 220°C/425°F/Gas 7 for 30 minutes and then at 180°C/350°F/Gas 4 for 20 minutes or until the fruit is tender.

### Wrapping larger fillings

Known as en croûte, wrapping meat or fish in pastry keeps it moist and succulent. Beef Wellington is a classic example, but a leg of lamb, whole salmon or even lamb cutlets can be cooked in this way. Brown the outside of larger cuts such as beef and lamb, then cool. Use about 450g/1lb rich shortcrust pastry or puff pastry for a 1.3kg/3lb fillet (tenderloin) of beef and 800g/1¾lb for a leg of lamb or medium-sized salmon.

**1** Roll out the pastry to the appropriate shape – for example, a rectangle for beef, a triangle for a leg of lamb – large enough to fully enclose the meat or fish. Wrap the meat or fish in the pastry. Seal the edges with a little water and put seam-side down on the baking sheet.

**2** Cut several steam holes in the pastry, then bake at 200°C/400°F/Gas 6 for the first 15 minutes, then at 180°C/350°F/Gas 4, until cooked – a meat thermometer is a good guide for this.

### Making pastry tubes

Little cannoli cylinders are used as moulds to shape and bake pastry. The pastry tubes can then be filled with cream or, in Sicilian tradition, ricotta cheese, nuts and candied fruit.

**1** Roll out 7.5cm/3in rounds of pâte sucrée into ovals the same length as the cannoli moulds. About 350g/12oz pastry will make eight tubes. Wrap each oval lengthways around a mould, sealing the join with egg white. Chill for 30 minutes.

**2** Deep-fry at 180°C/350°F until golden brown. Drain on kitchen paper, and remove from the moulds while hot.

## SHAPING FILO PASTRY

This paper-thin pastry is incredibly easy to shape into parcels and can be simply cut to the required size with a pair of scissors. It is also perfect for making large strudels, layered bakes and cooking en croûte, as well as making dainty baskets, purses and coils.

### Making a filo pastry roll

This is an excellent way to use filo pastry and combines well with sweet and spicy fruit fillings. Use 675g/1½lb of mixed chopped eating apples, dried fruit, sugar and spices.

**1** Using six sheets from a large packet of filo pastry, lay the first on a dishtowel, lightly brush with melted butter or oil, then place a second sheet on top. Continue to layer the filo, brushing butter between each layer.

**2** Spoon the filling over the pastry, leaving a 2.5cm/1in margin around the edges. Turn in the short pastry edges.

**3** With the help of the dishtowel, roll up from a long edge to enclose the filling. Brush with melted butter or oil and bake the pastry on a baking sheet at 180°C/350°F/Gas 4 for 30–40 minutes.

### Making filo baskets

Fresh summer fruits and rich seafood are equally delicious in these crisp filo cups. Invert ramekins on a baking sheet and grease with unsalted (sweet) butter. Cut filo pastry into 13cm/5in squares, brush each square with melted butter and drape four or five at angles over each mould. Bake at 180°C/350°F/Gas 4 for about 12 minutes. Cool, then lift the baskets off the moulds and fill.

### Making filo purses

Sometimes called money bags or swag bags, these parcels are simply made by drawing the pastry edges together and gently pinching the neck. Richly flavoured fillings, such as lightly cooked leeks with Roquefort cheese, work well.

Cut filo pastry into 13cm/5in squares. Lay three squares on top of each other, each at a slight angle to the other to make a 12-pointed star, brushing each layer with melted butter or oil. Spoon in a heaped teaspoon of filling, then pull the corners of the pastry up round it and pinch firmly to seal. Brush again with butter or oil and bake at 190°C/375°F/Gas 5 for 15 minutes.

### Making filo cocktail snacks

Filo pastry can be stacked in layers with a filling and baked before being cut into the required shape and size.

Layer three sheets of filo, brushing between with melted butter or oil. Spread thinly with the filling, then top with three more layers of buttered filo. With a sharp knife, mark the pastry into squares, fingers or diamonds. Bake at 180°C/350°F/Gas 4 for 20 minutes, then cut into bitesize pieces along the scored lines and serve hot or cold.

### Making filo triangles

Traditional Indian pasties, or samosas, are deep-fried filo triangles filled with a pre-cooked spiced meat or vegetable mixture. Other fillings such as chopped feta, prawns (shrimp) or chocolate can be made in the same way.

Fold filo sheets in half lengthways. Cut in half widthways, place a teaspoon of filling on the filo 5cm/2in from the end. Turn one corner over to make a triangle. Fold the triangle over on itself down the length of the filo. Seal the ends with melted butter or oil. Deep-fry in oil heated to 190°C/375°F for 4–5 minutes.

### Making spring rolls

Make these with spring roll wrappers or filo pastry. Keep the wrapping thin, so that you can just see the filling inside. Suitable fillings include beansprouts, water chestnuts, bamboo shoots with chopped prawns (shrimp) or finely minced (ground) pork.

Cut filo pastry into 13cm/5in squares and brush with oil. Place some filling in a strip about 2.5cm/1in from one side, leaving a 2cm/¾in margin at both ends. Fold the sides over the filling, then roll up, sealing the edge with beaten egg. Deep-fry in oil heated to 180°C/350°F.

## SHAPING PUFF PASTRY

Although puff pastry rises, it holds its shape well and is used for well-known pastry gâteaux such as mille-feuilles, as well as smaller sweet and savoury puff pastries, such as palmiers and mini pastry cases.

### Making puff pastry cases

Also known as vol-au-vents, these pastry cases can be made in many different sizes and can be stuffed with all sorts of fillings from hot garlic mushrooms to prawns (shrimp) in mayonnaise. When baked, the scored inner circle makes a lid that can be lifted out so that the pastry case can be filled. The smallest pastry cases are called "bouchées" meaning "mouthful" and are served as finger food.

To make bouchées, roll out puff pastry to a thickness of 5mm/¼in and stamp out rounds using a 4cm/1½in plain or fluted cutter. Transfer to a baking sheet and brush the tops with beaten egg. To make the lid, cut halfway through the depth of each round using a slightly smaller cutter. Chill, then bake at 220°C/425°F/Gas 7 for 12–15 minutes. Ease off the lid, scoop out any soft pastry, then fill. 450g/1lb puff pastry will yield about 25 bouchées.

### Making a large pastry case

Roll out 500g/1¼lb puff pastry and cut into a 23cm/9in round. Transfer to a baking sheet, then, using a side plate, score the pastry around it, but do not cut all the way through. Knock up the edges, chill, then bake at 230°C/450°F/Gas 8 for 25 minutes. Remove the lid and any soft pastry, then return the case to the oven for a few minutes, to dry.

### Making deep puff pastry cases

Both large and smaller individual puff pastry cases can be made deeper by placing a ring of pastry on top of the pastry round, so that more filling can be added. Rectangular, square or diamond shapes are also possible.

**1** To make individual deep round pastry cases, roll out the pastry to 5mm/¼in thick and stamp out rounds using a floured 10cm/4in cutter. Cut rings from half the pastry rounds, using a 7.5cm/3in cutter and discard the centres.

**2** Place the large rounds on a baking sheet and brush around the edges with beaten egg, then place a ring on top of each. Chill, brush the rings with beaten egg, and bake at 220°C/425°F/Gas 7 for 15–18 minutes until golden. Remove and discard the centres, or use as lids.

To make mini rectangular cases, roll out puff pastry to 7.5 x 10cm/3 x 4in rectangles, about 5mm/¼in thick. Cut an inner rectangle 2.5cm/1in from the pastry edge, scoring halfway through. Mark criss-cross lines on top of the inner rectangle, brush with egg and bake in a preheated oven at 220°C/425°F/Gas 7 for 12–15 minutes. Lift out the notched rectangles and use as lids.

### Making puff pastry layers

Mille-feuille, which means a thousand leaves, is the classic example of a layered puff pastry dessert. After baking, the rectangles of pastry are sandwiched together, usually with fruit and cream.

**1** Roll out 500g/1¼lb puff pastry to a 30 x 20cm/12 x 8in rectangle. Cut into three pieces, each 10 x 20cm/4 x 8in.

**2** Place on a baking sheet, cover and chill for 30 minutes. Brush with beaten egg, prick each piece, then bake in a preheated oven at 230°C/450°F/Gas 8 for 8–10 minutes. Cool and sandwich the layers together with the filling.

### Making feuilletées

These are a simple form of mille-feuille, usually made as single servings. Small rectangles of puff pastry are baked then split in half horizontally to form two layers. A filling, such as whipped cream and fruit is added, then the layers are sandwiched back together.

Roll out 350g/12oz puff pastry, 1cm/½in thick and cut into four 10 x 6cm/4 x 2½in rectangles. Chill for 20 minutes, then brush with beaten egg and bake in a preheated oven at 220°C/425°F/Gas 7 for 12–15 minutes.

### Shaping palmiers

These pastries are a Parisian speciality. While they are often simply rolled in sugar, they may have a nut filling of chopped almonds, walnuts or hazelnuts mixed with ground cinnamon and sugar.

**1** Lightly sprinkle the work surface with caster (superfine) sugar and roll out 225g/8oz puff or rough puff pastry to a 50 × 20cm/20 × 8in rectangle.

**2** Brush with beaten egg, then sprinkle evenly with half the nut mixture.

**3** Fold in the long edges of the pastry to meet in the centre and flatten with the rolling pin. Brush the top with egg and sprinkle with three-quarters of the nut mixture. Fold in the edges again to meet in the centre, brush with egg and sprinkle with the remaining nut mixture. Fold half the pastry over the other.

**4** Cut crossways into 2cm/¾in thick slices and place, cut-side down, about 2.5cm/1in apart on greased baking sheets. Slightly open up the pastries.

**5** Bake in a preheated oven at 220°C/425°F/Gas 7 for 8–10 minutes until golden, carefully turning the palmiers over halfway through the cooking time.

### Making coiled puff pastry cones

Strips of puff pastry are easily coiled around metal cornet moulds then baked to make cones ready to be filled with flavoured whipped cream. To make a rich savoury version, prepare the cones without the sugar coating, and fill with a piped mixture of pâté and butter.

**1** Roll out 225g/8oz puff pastry to a 56 × 15cm/22 × 6in rectangle. Starting at one short end, roll up tightly. Cut the roll into 1cm/½in coiled slices.

**2** Unroll each coil and dampen the ends of each strip with water. Wrap the pastry around a lightly greased metal cornet mould in a spiral, starting at the pointed end and overlapping it slightly. At the wide end, press the pastry strip firmly to secure.

**3** Chill on a baking sheet, with the finished ends underneath, for about 30 minutes. Brush with beaten egg and sprinkle with caster (superfine) sugar. Bake in a preheated oven at 220°C/425°F/Gas 7 for 8–10 minutes.

**4** Cool the pastries on the baking sheet for 5 minutes, then remove from the moulds. Cool completely, before piping in flavoured whipped cream.

### Gâteau Pithiviers

This scored-top pastry originates from the town of the same name, near Paris. It has a rum-flavoured almond filling and is recognized by the spiral pattern on the pastry lid.

**1** Roll out two 25cm/10in rounds from 500g/1¼lb puff pastry. Place one on a baking sheet. Mix 50g/2oz/¼ cup butter, 115g/4oz/1 cup sifted icing (confectioners') sugar, 115g/4oz/1 cup ground almonds, 2 egg yolks and 30ml/2 tbsp rum in a bowl, and spread over the pastry round leaving a border of 2.5cm/1in all round.

**2** Brush the border with water and top with the second pastry round, pressing to seal the edges. Knock up and scallop the edge.

**3** With a knife, mark curved lines 5mm/¼in apart, from the centre to the edge and cutting only halfway through the pastry. Cover with clear film (plastic wrap) and chill for 30 minutes. Glaze, then bake in a preheated oven at 230°C/450°F/Gas 8 for 25 minutes.

# SAVOURY PASTRIES AND TARTS

*An inspirational collection of savoury tarts that will taste better than any you can buy. Included here are all-time favourites such as hearty Cornish Pasties and Quiche Lorraine, with its creamy egg-rich custard. Discover some wonderful variations on the classic quiche, with all manner of fillings. As delicious as it is, shortcrust isn't the only pastry used here; puff, filo, hot water crust and cornmeal pastries all make wonderful tarts, parcels and pies.*

# MINI PORK AND BACON PIES

*THESE LITTLE PIES CAN BE MADE UP TO A DAY AHEAD OF BEING SERVED. THEY ARE A GOOD CHOICE FOR A SUMMER PICNIC OR SPECIAL PACKED LUNCH FOR SCHOOL OR THE OFFICE.*

MAKES TWELVE

INGREDIENTS
 10ml/2 tsp sunflower oil
 1 onion, chopped
 225g/8oz pork, coarsely chopped
 115g/4oz cooked bacon, finely diced
 45ml/3 tbsp chopped fresh herbs,
  such as sage, parsley and oregano
 6 eggs, hard-boiled and halved
 1 egg yolk, beaten
 20g/¾oz packet powdered aspic
 300ml/½ pint/1¼ cups boiling water
 salt and ground black pepper
For the hot water crust pastry
 450g/1lb/4 cups plain
  (all-purpose) flour
 115g/4oz/½ cup white vegetable fat
 275ml/9fl oz/generous 1 cup water

**1** To make the pastry, sift the flour into a bowl and add a good pinch each of salt and pepper. Gently heat the fat and water in a large pan until the fat has melted. Increase the heat and bring the mixture to the boil. Pour the hot liquid into the flour, stirring constantly.

**2** Press the mixture into a ball of dough using a spoon. When the dough is smooth, cover the bowl and set aside.

**3** Preheat the oven to 200°C/400°F/ Gas 6. Heat the oil in a frying pan, add the onion and cook until soft. Stir in the pork and bacon and cook until just brown. Remove from the heat and stir in the herbs and seasoning.

**4** Roll out two-thirds of the pastry on a lightly floured surface. Use a 12cm/4½in fluted cutter to stamp out rounds and use to line 12 muffin pans. Place some of the meat mixture in each pie, then add half an egg to each and top with the remaining meat mixture.

**5** Roll out the remaining pastry and use a 7.5cm/3in fluted cutter to stamp out lids for the pies. Dampen the rim of each pastry base and press a lid in place. Pinch the edges to seal. Brush with egg yolk and make a small steam hole in the top of each pie.

**6** Bake for 30–35 minutes. Leave the pies to cool for 15 minutes, then place on a wire rack to cool completely.

**7** Meanwhile, stir the aspic powder into the boiling water until dissolved. Shape a piece of foil into a small funnel and use this to guide a little aspic through the hole in the top of each pie.

**8** Leave to cool and set, then chill the pies for up to 24 hours before serving at room temperature.

# CORNISH PASTIES

*THESE TRADITIONAL PASTRIES ARE MADE WITH A RICH CRUMBLY SHORTCRUST. THE FILLING IS RAW WHEN ENCLOSED IN THE PASTRY, SO THEY MUST BE COOKED THOROUGHLY.*

MAKES SIX

INGREDIENTS
  450g/1lb chuck steak, diced
  1 potato, about 175g/6oz, diced
  175g/6oz swede (rutabaga), diced
  1 onion, chopped
  2.5ml/½ tsp dried mixed herbs
  1 egg, beaten
  salt and ground black pepper
  salad, to garnish
For the shortcrust pastry
  350g/12oz/3 cups plain
    (all-purpose) flour
  pinch of salt
  115g/4oz/½ cup butter, diced
  50g/2oz/¼ cup lard or white
    vegetable fat
  75–90ml/5–6 tbsp chilled water

**1** To make the pastry, sift the flour and salt into a bowl. Using your fingertips or a pastry blender, lightly rub or cut in the butter and lard or vegetable fat, then sprinkle over most of the chilled water and mix to a soft dough, adding more water if necessary. Knead the pastry on a lightly floured surface for a few seconds until smooth. Wrap in clear film (plastic wrap) and chill for 30 minutes.

**2** Preheat the oven to 220°C/425°F/ Gas 7. Divide the pastry into six pieces, then roll out each piece on a lightly floured surface to a 20cm/8in round.

**3** Mix together the steak, vegetables, herbs and seasoning in a bowl, then spoon an equal amount on to one half of each pastry round.

**4** Brush the pastry edges with water, then fold the free half of each round over the filling. Press the edges firmly together to seal, then use your fingertips to crimp the edges.

**5** Brush the pasties with the beaten egg. Bake for 15 minutes, then reduce the temperature to 160°C/325°F/Gas 3 and bake for 1 hour more. Serve the pasties hot or cold with a salad garnish.

# ALSACE LEEK AND ONION TARTLETS

*THE SAVOURY FILLING IN THESE TARTLETS IS TRADITIONAL TO NORTH-EASTERN FRANCE, WHERE MANY TYPES OF QUICHE ARE POPULAR. BAKING THE TARTS IN INDIVIDUAL TINS MAKES FOR EASIER SERVING — AND THEY LOOK ATTRACTIVE ON THE PLATE, ACCOMPANIED WITH A SALAD GARNISH.*

SERVES SIX

INGREDIENTS
  25g/1oz/2 tbsp butter
  1 onion, thinly sliced
  2.5ml/½ tsp dried thyme
  450g/1lb leeks, thinly sliced
  50g/2oz/½ cup grated Gruyère or
    Emmenthal cheese
  3 eggs
  300ml/½pint/1¼ cups single
    (light) cream
  pinch of freshly grated nutmeg
  salt and ground black pepper
  salad, to serve
For the rich shortcrust pastry
  175g/6oz/1½ cups plain
    (all-purpose) flour
  75g/3oz/6 tbsp cold butter, diced
  1 egg yolk
  30–45m/2–3 tbsp chilled water
  2.5m/½ tsp salt

**1** To make the pastry, sift the flour into a bowl and add the butter. Cut in the butter using a pastry blender or rub in the flour with your fingertips until the mixture resembles fine breadcrumbs.

**2** Make a well in the centre of the flour mixture. Beat together the egg yolk, chilled water and salt in a small bowl. Pour into the well in the dry ingredients and, using a fork, mix the flour and liquid until they begin to stick together and a soft, pliable dough is formed. Shape into a flattened ball. Wrap the dough in clear film (plastic wrap) and chill for about 30 minutes.

**3** Lightly butter six 10cm/4in tartlet tins (mini quiche pans). Roll out the dough on a lightly floured surface until about 3mm/⅛in thick, then, using a 12.5cm/5in plain cutter, cut as many rounds as possible. Gently ease the pastry rounds into the tins, pressing the pastry firmly along the base and sides. Re-roll the trimmings and line the remaining tins. Prick the bases. Chill for 30 minutes.

**4** Preheat the oven to 190°C/375°F/Gas 5. Line the pastry cases with foil and fill with baking beans, making sure they are evenly distributed over the pastry bases. Place the pastry cases on a baking sheet.

**5** Bake for 6–8 minutes until the edges of the pastry are golden. Lift out the foil and beans and return the partially baked pastry cases to the oven. Bake for 2 minutes more or until the bases are dry. Transfer the pastry cases in their tins to a wire rack to cool. Reduce the oven temperature to 180°C/350°F/Gas 4.

**6** Place the butter in a large frying pan, and melt over a medium heat, then add the onion and thyme and cook for about 5 minutes until the onion is soft and translucent, stirring often.

**7** Add the sliced leeks and cook for about 10 minutes until they are soft and tender. Divide the mixture evenly among the pastry cases and sprinkle each with cheese, dividing it evenly.

**8** Beat the eggs, cream, nutmeg and salt and pepper together in a small mixing bowl until well mixed. Place the pastry cases in their tins on a baking sheet and pour in the egg mixture, evenly covering the leek filling. Bake the tartlets for 15–20 minutes until set and golden.

**9** Transfer the tartlet tins to a wire rack to cool slightly and allow the pastry to firm up a little. Remove the tartlets from the tins and lift them on to individual plates. Serve warm or at room temperature with a salad garnish.

# PROSCIUTTO AND MOZZARELLA PARCELS

*IN THESE TASTY LITTLE PARCELS, THE MOZZARELLA IS ADDED AS MUCH FOR ITS TEXTURE THAN ITS FLAVOUR. BITE INTO THESE CRISP FILO PARCELS TO REVEAL A CREAMY MELTED CHEESE AND HAM FILLING.*

SERVES SIX

INGREDIENTS
a little hot chilli sauce
6 prosciutto slices, such as
Parma ham
200g/7oz mozzarella cheese, cut into
6 slices
6 sheets of filo pastry, each
measuring 45 × 28cm/18 × 11in,
thawed if frozen
50g/2oz/¼ cup butter, melted

**COOK'S TIP**
Parma ham is readily available, usually along with at least one other type of prosciutto. Visit a good Italian deli and you will find a choice of regional hams.

**1** Preheat the oven to 200°C/400°F/ Gas 6. Sprinkle a little of the hot chilli sauce over each slice of prosciutto. Place a slice of mozzarella in the centre of each piece of prosciutto, then fold the ends of the ham around the cheese to meet neatly in the middle.

**2** Brush a sheet of filo pastry with a little melted butter. Fold in half lengthways and brush the top with butter. Wrap a ham and mozzarella parcel in the pastry to make a package, tucking the edges in neatly as you go. Place on a baking sheet, seam side down, and brush with a little more butter. Repeat with the remaining ham and cheese parcels and pastry sheets.

**3** Bake the filo parcels for 15 minutes, or until the pastry is crisp and evenly golden. Serve all together or arrange on individual plates, with a frisée salad, if you wish. Serve immediately.

# SMOKED CHICKEN WITH PEACH MAYONNAISE IN FILO TARTLETS

*THE FILLING FOR THESE CHICKEN TARTLETS CAN BE PREPARED A DAY IN ADVANCE AND CHILLED, BUT DO NOT FILL THE PASTRY CASES UNTIL YOU ARE READY TO SERVE THEM OR THEY WILL BECOME SOGGY.*

MAKES TWELVE

INGREDIENTS
25g/1oz/2 tbsp butter
3 sheets of filo pastry, each
measuring 45 × 28cm/18 × 11in,
thawed if frozen
2 skinless, boneless smoked chicken
breast portions, finely sliced
150ml/¼ pint/⅔ cup mayonnaise
grated rind of 1 lime
30ml/2 tbsp lime juice
2 ripe peaches, peeled, stoned
(pitted) and chopped
salt and ground black pepper
fresh tarragon sprigs, lime slices
and salad leaves, to garnish

**1** Preheat the oven to 200°C/400°F/ Gas 6. Place the butter in a small pan and heat gently until melted. Lightly brush 12 mini flan rings with a little melted butter.

**2** Cut each sheet of filo pastry into 12 equal rounds large enough to line the tins and stand above the rims. Place a round of pastry in each tin and brush with a little butter, then add another round of pastry. Brush each with more butter and add a third round of pastry.

**3** Bake the tartlets for 5 minutes. Leave in the tins for a few moments before transferring to a wire rack to cool.

**4** Mix together the chicken, mayonnaise, lime rind, peaches and seasoning. Chill for at least 30 minutes, but preferably overnight. When ready to serve, spoon the chicken mixture into the filo pastry cases and garnish with tarragon sprigs, lime slices and salad leaves.

**COOK'S TIP**
Use small tartlet tins (mini quiche pans) if you don't have mini flan rings.

# SHELLFISH <u>IN</u> PUFF PASTRY

*WITH A COASTLINE BORDERING TWO SEAS AND A VAST NETWORK OF RIVERS, FISH AND SHELLFISH PLAY A LEADING ROLE IN FRENCH CUISINE. THIS CLASSIC COMBINATION OF SHELLFISH IN A CREAMY SAUCE SERVED IN A PUFF PASTRY CASE IS FOUND ON THE MENUS OF MANY ELEGANT RESTAURANTS IN FRANCE.*

SERVES SIX

INGREDIENTS
  350g/12oz rough puff or
    puff pastry
  1 egg beaten with 15ml/1 tbsp water
  60ml/4 tbsp dry white wine
  2 shallots, finely chopped
  450g/1lb mussels, scrubbed and
    beards removed
  15g/½oz/1 tbsp butter
  450g/1lb shelled scallops,
    halved crossways
  450g/1lb raw prawns (shrimp), peeled
  225g/8oz/1 cup butter, diced
  2 shallots, finely chopped
  250ml/8fl oz/1 cup fish stock
  90ml/6 tbsp dry white wine
  15–30ml/1–2 tbsp single
    (light) cream
  lemon juice
  175g/6oz cooked lobster meat, sliced
  salt and ground white pepper
  fresh dill sprigs, to garnish

**1** Lightly grease a large baking sheet and sprinkle it with a little water. Roll out the pastry on a lightly floured surface into a rectangle slightly less than 5mm/¼in thick. Using a sharp knife, cut into six diamond shapes about 13cm/5in long. Transfer to the baking sheet, spacing them well.

**2** Brush each diamond with the egg and water mixture to glaze. Using the tip of a knife, score a line around each diamond 1cm/½in from the edge, then lightly cross hatch. Chill for 30 minutes.

**3** Preheat the oven to 220°C/425°F/Gas 7. Bake the pastry cases for about 20 minutes until puffed and brown. Carefully remove each lid, cutting along the scored line. Scoop out and discard any uncooked dough, then leave the cases and lids to cool completely.

**4** Place the white wine and shallots in a large pan and bring to the boil. Add the mussels, cover tightly and cook for about 5 minutes until the shells open, shaking the pan occasionally. Discard any mussels that do not open.

**5** Reserve six mussels for the garnish. Remove the rest from their shells and set aside in a bowl covered with cling film (plastic wrap). Strain the cooking liquid through a muslin- (cheesecloth-) lined sieve and reserve for the sauce.

**6** Melt the butter in a heavy frying pan. Add the scallops and prawns, cover tightly and cook for 3–4 minutes until they feel just firm to the touch; take care you do not overcook them.

**7** Using a slotted spoon, transfer the scallops and prawns to the bowl with the mussels and add any cooking juices to the mussel liquid.

**8** Melt half the butter in a heavy pan and cook the shallots for 2 minutes, stirring. Pour in the fish stock and boil for about 15 minutes until it is reduced by three-quarters. Add the white wine and the reserved mussel liquid and boil for 5–7 minutes until reduced by half.

**9** Lower the heat and whisk in the remaining butter, a little at a time, to make a smooth, thick sauce. Whisk in the cream and season with a little salt, if needed, white pepper and lemon juice. Keep warm over a very low heat, stirring frequently.

**10** Warm the pastry cases and lids in the oven set at a low temperature for 10 minutes. Put the mussels, scallops and prawns in a large pan. Stir in a quarter of the sauce and reheat gently. Fold in the lobster meat and cook for 1 minute more.

**11** Arrange the puff pastry cases on individual plates. Divide the shellfish mixture equally among them and top with the lids. Garnish each with one of the reserved mussels and a dill sprig and spoon the remaining sauce around the edges or serve separately.

# COURGETTE <u>AND</u> DILL TART

*THE SUBTLE FLAVOUR OF COURGETTES IS LIFTED DRAMATICALLY BY THE ADDITION OF FRESH DILL IN THIS TART. TAKE TIME TO ARRANGE THE COURGETTE LAYERS TO CREATE AN EYE-CATCHING DISH.*

**4** Roll out the pastry and ease it into the tin. Prick the base, trim the edges and bake blind for 10–15 minutes.

**5** Meanwhile, heat the oil in a frying pan, add the courgettes and sauté for 2–3 minutes until lightly browned, turning occasionally. Mix the egg yolks, cream, garlic and dill in a small bowl. Season with salt and pepper.

**6** Line the pastry case with courgettes and pour over the cream mixture. Return to the oven for 25–30 minutes and bake until firm. Cool the pie in the tin, then remove and serve.

SERVES FOUR

INGREDIENTS
  15ml/1 tbsp sunflower oil
  3 courgettes (zucchini), thinly sliced
  2 egg yolks
  150ml/¼ pint/⅔ cup double
    (heavy) cream
  1 garlic clove, crushed
  15ml/1 tbsp finely chopped fresh dill
  salt and ground black pepper
For the shortcrust pastry
  115g/4oz/1 cup wholemeal
    (whole-wheat) flour
  115g/4oz/1 cup self-raising
    (self-rising) flour
  pinch of salt
  115g/4oz/½ cup butter, chilled
    and diced
  75ml/5 tbsp chilled water

**1** To make the pastry, sift the flours into a bowl, tipping the bran into the bowl, then place in a food processor. Add the salt and diced butter and process using the pulse button until the mixture resembles fine breadcrumbs.

**2** With the motor running, gradually add the water until the mixture forms a dough. Do not over-process. Wrap the pastry and chill for 30 minutes.

**3** Preheat the oven to 200°C/400°F/ Gas 6 and grease a 20cm/8in flan tin (quiche pan).

**COOK'S TIP**
The smaller and skinnier courgettes are, the better they taste. Choose ones that have glossy green skins and feel firm.

# QUICHE LORRAINE

*THIS CLASSIC QUICHE HAS SOME DELIGHTFUL CHARACTERISTICS THAT ARE OFTEN FORGOTTEN IN MODERN RECIPES; NAMELY VERY THIN PASTRY, A CREAMY, LIGHT FILLING AND SMOKED BACON.*

### SERVES FOUR TO SIX

INGREDIENTS

6 rindless smoked streaky (fatty) bacon rashers (strips)
300ml/½ pint/1¼ cups double (heavy) cream
3 eggs, plus 2 yolks
25g/1oz/2 tbsp butter
salt and ground black pepper

For the rich shortcrust pastry

175g/6oz/1½ cups plain (all-purpose) flour, sifted
pinch of salt
115g/4oz/½ cup butter, at room temperature, diced
1 egg yolk

**1** To make the pastry, place the flour, salt, butter and egg yolk in a food processor and process until blended. Tip out on to a lightly floured surface and bring the mixture together into a ball. Leave to rest for 20 minutes.

**2** Lightly flour a deep 20cm/8in round flan tin (quiche pan) and place it on a baking sheet. Roll out the pastry and use to line the flan tin, trimming off any overhanging pieces.

**3** Gently press the pastry into the corners of the tin. If the pastry breaks, gently push it together again. Chill for 20 minutes. Preheat the oven to 200°C/400°F/Gas 6.

**4** Meanwhile, snip the bacon into small pieces using kitchen scissors and grill (broil) until the fat runs. Arrange in the pastry case. Beat together the cream, the eggs and yolks and seasoning, and pour into the pastry case.

**5** Bake the quiche for 15 minutes, then reduce the oven temperature to 180°C/350°F/Gas 4 and bake for 20 minutes more. When the filling is puffed up and golden brown and the pastry edge crisp, remove the quiche from the oven and top with small cubes of butter. Leave to stand for 5 minutes before serving. This allows the filling to settle and cool a little before serving, making it easier to cut the quiche.

**COOK'S TIP**
To prepare the quiche in advance, bake for 5–10 minutes less than the time stated, until the filling is just set. Reheat at 190°C/375°F/Gas 5 for 10 minutes.

# RED ONION TART <u>WITH A</u> CORNMEAL CRUST

*THE WONDERFULLY MILD AND SWEET TASTE OF RED ONIONS WHEN COOKED GOES PERFECTLY WITH FONTINA CHEESE AND THYME IN THIS TART. CORNMEAL GIVES THE PASTRY A CRUMBLY TEXTURE.*

SERVES FIVE TO SIX

INGREDIENTS

   60ml/4 tbsp olive oil
   1kg/2¼lb red onions, thinly sliced
   2–3 garlic cloves, thinly sliced
   5ml/1 tsp chopped fresh thyme, plus
     a few whole sprigs
   5ml/1 tsp soft dark brown sugar
   10ml/2 tsp sherry vinegar
   225g/8oz Fontina cheese,
     thinly sliced
   salt and ground black pepper
For the cornmeal pastry
   115g/4oz/1 cup plain
     (all-purpose) flour
   75g/3oz/¾ cup fine yellow cornmeal
   5ml/1 tsp soft dark brown sugar
   5ml/1 tsp chopped fresh thyme
   90g/3½oz/7 tbsp butter, diced
   1 egg yolk
   30–45ml/2–3 tbsp chilled water

**1** To make the pastry, sift the flour and cornmeal with 5ml/1 tsp salt in a bowl. Add plenty of black pepper and stir in the sugar and thyme. Rub or cut in the butter until the mixture resembles fine breadcrumbs. Beat the egg yolk with 30ml/2 tbsp water and use to bind the pastry, adding more water if necessary. Gather into a ball, wrap in clear film (plastic wrap) and chill for 30 minutes.

**2** To make the filling, heat 45ml/3 tbsp of the oil in a large, deep frying pan and add the onions. Cover and cook slowly, stirring occasionally, for 20–30 minutes.

**3** Add the garlic and chopped thyme and cook, stirring occasionally, for about 10 minutes. Increase the heat slightly, then add the sugar and sherry vinegar. Cook, uncovered, for another 5 minutes until the onions start to caramelize slightly. Season and cool.

**4** Preheat the oven to 190°C/375°F/ Gas 5. Roll out the pastry thinly and use to line a 25cm/10in loose-based flan tin (quiche pan). Prick the pastry all over with a fork and support the sides with foil. Bake for 12–15 minutes until the pastry is just lightly coloured.

**5** Remove the foil and spread the onions in the base of the pastry case. Add the Fontina and season to taste. Drizzle over the remaining oil, then bake for 15–20 minutes until the filling is hot. Garnish with a few thyme sprigs and serve immediately.

# ROQUEFORT TART WITH WALNUT PASTRY

*MILD LEEKS GO EXCEPTIONALLY WELL WITH THE SALTY FLAVOUR OF THE ROQUEFORT CHEESE, AND THE NUTTINESS OF THE PASTRY COMPLEMENTS THE INGREDIENTS PERFECTLY IN THIS TART.*

SERVES FOUR TO SIX

INGREDIENTS
25g/1oz/2 tbsp butter
450g/1lb leeks (trimmed weight), sliced
175g/6oz Roquefort cheese, sliced
2 large eggs
250ml/8fl oz/1 cup double (heavy) cream
10ml/2 tsp chopped fresh tarragon
salt and ground black pepper
For the walnut pastry
175g/6oz/1½ cups plain (all-purpose) flour
5ml/1 tsp soft dark brown sugar
50g/2oz/¼ cup butter, diced
75g/3oz/¾ cup walnuts, ground
15ml/1 tbsp lemon juice
30ml/2 tbsp chilled water

**1** To make the pastry, sift the flour and 2.5ml/½ tsp salt into a bowl. Add some black pepper and the sugar. Rub or cut in the butter until the mixture resembles fine breadcrumbs, then add the ground walnuts and stir well. Add the lemon juice and chilled water and bind to form a dough. Gather the mixture into a ball, wrap in clear film (plastic wrap) and chill for 30–40 minutes.

**2** Preheat the oven to 190°C/375°F/Gas 5. Roll out the pastry and use to line a 21–23cm/8½–9in loose-based flan tin (quiche pan).

**COOK'S TIP**
To prepare the walnuts, mix with a little of the pastry flour and use a small food processor or clean coffee mill to grind.

**3** Protect the sides of the pastry case with a thin strip of foil, prick the base all over with a fork and bake for about 15 minutes. Remove the foil and bake the pastry case for 10 minutes more until just firm to the touch. Reduce the oven temperature to 180°C/350°F/Gas 4.

**4** To make the filling, melt the butter in a pan, add the leeks, then cover and cook for 10 minutes. Season and cook for a further 10 minutes until soft. Set aside to cool.

**5** Spoon the leeks into the pastry case, spreading them evenly, and arrange the slices of Roquefort cheese on top. Beat the eggs with the cream in a small bowl, and season with plenty of black pepper. Beat in the tarragon and carefully pour the mixture into the pastry case, evenly covering the leek filling.

**6** Bake the tart on the centre shelf of the oven for 30–40 minutes until the filling has risen and browned and become firm to the touch. Allow to cool for 10 minutes before serving.

# HERBED GREEK MINI TARTS

*IF YOU CAN, USE LARGE MUFFIN PANS TO MAKE THESE LITTLE PIES. THEY PROVIDE A DEEP CASE TO HOLD PLENTY OF THE DELICIOUSLY TANGY YOGURT FILLING.*

MAKES EIGHT

INGREDIENTS
   45–60ml/3–4 tbsp tapenade or
     sun-dried tomato paste
   1 large egg
   100g/3¾oz/scant ½ cup thick Greek
     (US strained plain) yogurt
   90ml/6 tbsp milk
   1 garlic clove, crushed
   30ml/2 tbsp chopped mixed herbs,
     such as thyme, marjoram, basil
     and parsley
   salt and ground black pepper
For the shortcrust pastry
   115g/4oz/1 cup plain
     (all-purpose) flour
   pinch of salt
   50g/2oz/¼ cup butter, diced
   30ml/2 tbsp chilled water

**1** To make the pastry, sift the flour and salt into a large bowl. Rub or cut in the butter. Sprinkle over the water and mix to a dough. Knead briefly, then wrap and chill for 20 minutes.

**2** Roll out the pastry and cut out eight rounds. Use to line deep muffin pans.

**3** Chill the pastry cases for 30 minutes. Meanwhile, preheat the oven to 190°C/375°F/Gas 5. Line each pastry case with a small piece of foil. Bake for about 15 minutes. Remove the foil and bake for a further 5 minutes or until the cases are crisp and dry.

**4** Spread a little tapenade or tomato paste in the base of each pastry case. Whisk together the egg, yogurt, milk, garlic, herbs and seasoning.

**5** Carefully spoon the egg mixture into the pastry cases and bake for about 30 minutes, or until the filling is just firm to the touch and the pastry golden. Allow the pies to cool slightly before carefully removing them from the pans and serving.

# TOMATO AND BLACK OLIVE TART

*THIS DELICIOUS TART HAS A FRESH, RICH MEDITERRANEAN FLAVOUR AND IS PERFECT FOR PICNICS. IF YOU ARE TAKING THIS TART ON A PICNIC, KEEP IN THE TIN FOR EASY TRANSPORTING.*

SERVES EIGHT

INGREDIENTS
   6 firm plum tomatoes
   75g/3oz ripe Brie cheese
   about 16 pitted black olives
   3 eggs, beaten
   300ml/½ pint/1¼ cups milk
   30ml/2 tbsp chopped fresh herbs
   salt and ground black pepper
For the shortcrust pastry
   225g/8oz/2 cups plain
     (all-purpose) flour
   115g/4oz/½ cup butter, diced
   45–60ml/3–4 tbsp chilled water

**1** To make the pastry, sift the flour into a mixing bowl and rub or cut in the butter until the mixture resembles fine breadcrumbs. Sprinkle over the water and mix to a dough. Knead lightly on a floured surface for a few seconds until smooth. Wrap and chill for 30 minutes.

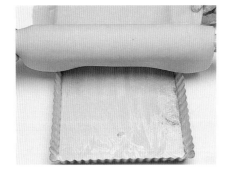

**2** Preheat the oven to 190°C/375°F/Gas 5. Roll out the pastry thinly and use to line a greased 28 x 18cm/11 x 7in loose-based rectangular flan tin (quiche pan). Trim the edges.

**3** Line the pastry case with some foil and baking beans, and bake blind for 15 minutes. Remove the foil and beans and bake for a further 5 minutes until the base is crisp.

**4** Slice the tomatoes, cube the cheese and finely slice the olives. Place the flan case on a baking sheet and arrange the tomatoes, cheese and olives in it. Mix together the eggs, milk, seasoning and chopped herbs.

**5** Pour the egg mixture into the case. Bake for about 40 minutes until just firm and turning golden. Slice hot or cool in the tin, then serve.

# VEGETARIAN FESTIVE TART

*THIS SOPHISTICATED FLAN MADE WITH A SPICY CHEESE PASTRY CAN BE SERVED AS A VEGETARIAN ALTERNATIVE FOR ANY CELEBRATION OR SPECIAL OCCASION.*

SERVES EIGHT

INGREDIENTS
    25g/1oz/2 tbsp butter
    1 onion, finely chopped
    1–2 garlic cloves, crushed
    350g/12oz/4–5 cups mushrooms,
      roughly chopped
    10ml/2 tsp dried mixed herbs
    15ml/1 tbsp chopped fresh parsley
    50g/2oz/1 cup fresh white
      breadcrumbs
    15ml/1 tbsp Dijon mustard
    salt and ground black pepper
For the spicy cheese pastry
    225g/8oz/2 cups plain
      (all-purpose) flour
    175g/6oz/¾ cup butter
    10ml/2 tsp paprika
    115g/4oz Parmesan cheese, grated
    1 egg, beaten with 15ml/1 tbsp
      chilled water
For the cheese topping
    25g/1oz/2 tbsp butter
    25g/1oz/2 tbsp plain flour
    300ml/½ pint/1¼ cups milk
    25g/1oz Parmesan
      cheese, grated
    75g/3oz Cheddar cheese, grated
    1.5ml/¼ tsp English
      mustard powder
    1 egg, separated

**1** To make the pastry, sift the flour into a bowl and rub or cut in the butter until it resembles fine breadcrumbs. Stir in the paprika and Parmesan cheese. Bind to a soft dough with the egg and water. Knead until smooth, wrap in clear film (plastic wrap) and chill for 30 minutes.

**2** To make the filling, melt the butter in a pan, add the onion and cook until tender. Add the garlic and mushrooms and cook, uncovered, for 5 minutes, stirring occasionally. Increase the heat to evaporate any liquid in the pan. Remove the pan from the heat and stir in the herbs, white breadcrumbs and seasoning. Allow to cool. Preheat the oven to 190°C/375°F/Gas 5, with a baking sheet placed inside.

**3** On a lightly floured surface, roll out the pastry and use to line a 23cm/9in loose-based flan tin (quiche pan), pressing it into the edges and making a narrow rim around the top. Chill.

**4** To make the cheese topping, melt the butter in a pan, stir in the flour and cook for 2 minutes. Gradually blend in the milk. Bring to the boil, stirring constantly, and simmer for 2–3 minutes. Remove the pan from the heat and stir in the cheeses, mustard powder and egg yolk, and season. Beat vigorously until smooth. Whisk the egg white until it holds soft peaks, then fold into the cheese mixture.

**5** Spread the mustard evenly over the pastry case. Spoon in the mushroom filling and then pour over the cheese topping. Bake on the hot baking sheet for 35–45 minutes until golden.

# SHALLOT AND GARLIC TARTE TATIN

*SAVOURY VERSIONS OF THE CELEBRATED APPLE TARTE TATIN HAVE BEEN POPULAR FOR SOME YEARS. HERE, CARAMELIZED SHALLOTS ARE BAKED BENEATH A LAYER OF PARMESAN PASTRY.*

SERVES FOUR TO SIX

INGREDIENTS
   300g/11oz puff pastry
   50g/2oz/¼ cup butter, softened
   75g/3oz/1 cup freshly grated
      Parmesan cheese
For the topping
   40g/1½oz/3 tbsp butter
   500g/1¼lb shallots
   12–16 large garlic cloves, peeled but
      left whole
   15ml/1 tbsp caster (superfine) sugar
   15ml/1 tbsp balsamic or
      sherry vinegar
   45ml/3 tbsp water
   5ml/1 tsp chopped fresh thyme
   salt and ground black pepper

**1**  Roll out the pastry to a rectangle on a lightly floured work surface. Spread the butter over it, leaving a 2.5cm/1in border. Sprinkle the grated Parmesan on top.

**2**  Fold the lower third of the pastry up to cover the middle and fold the top third down over it. Seal the edges well, give the pastry a quarter turn and roll it out to a rectangle, then fold in thirds and seal as before. Wrap in clear film (plastic wrap) and chill in the refrigerator for at least 30 minutes.

**3**  Preheat the oven to 190°C/375°F/ Gas 5. Melt the butter in a 23–25cm/ 9–10in round, heavy, ovenproof omelette pan. Add the shallots and garlic and cook over a low heat until lightly browned all over.

**4**  Sprinkle the sugar over and increase the heat a little. Cook until the sugar begins to caramelize, then stir. Add the vinegar, water, thyme and seasoning. Cook, partly covered, for 5–8 minutes until the garlic cloves are just tender. Set aside to cool.

**5**  Roll out the pastry to a round the same size as the omelette pan. Lay the pastry round over the shallots and garlic. Prick the pastry, then bake for 25–35 minutes until risen and golden. Cool for about 10 minutes, then invert the tart on to a serving platter.

# SINGLE- AND DOUBLE-CRUST PIES

Comforting and substantial main-course pies are always welcome.

Winter chills are warded off with a classic Steak and Kidney Pie with

a contemporary mustard gravy, while summer specials include a

mouthwatering Chicken and Apricot Filo Pie. At Christmas or

Thanksgiving, a Turkey and Cranberry Pie would make a stunning

centrepiece, as would a vegetarian Potato and Leek Filo Pie.

# CHICKEN CHARTER PIE

*THIS IS A TRADITIONAL RECIPE FROM CORNWALL, IN ENGLAND, AN AREA FAMOUS FOR ITS CLOTTED CREAM. IT IS NOT SURPRISING, THEREFORE, THAT THE SAUCE FOR THIS PIE IS CREAM-BASED.*

SERVES FOUR

INGREDIENTS
  50g/2oz/¼ cup butter
  4 chicken legs
  1 onion, finely chopped
  150ml/¼ pint/⅔ cup milk
  150ml/¼ pint/⅔ cup sour cream
  4 spring onions (scallions),
    quartered
  20g/¾oz/¾ cup fresh parsley leaves,
    finely chopped
  225g/8oz puff pastry
  2 eggs, beaten, plus extra for glazing
  120ml/4fl oz/½ cup double
    (heavy) cream
  salt and ground black pepper

**1** Melt the butter in a heavy, shallow pan, then brown the chicken legs on all sides. Transfer to a plate.

**2** Add the chopped onion to the pan and cook until just softened but not browned. Stir in the milk, sour cream, spring onions, parsley and seasoning. Bring to the boil, then simmer for 2 minutes.

**3** Return the chicken to the pan with any juices, cover tightly and cook very gently for about 30 minutes. Transfer the chicken and sauce mixture to a 1.2 litre/2 pint/5 cup pie dish and leave to cool.

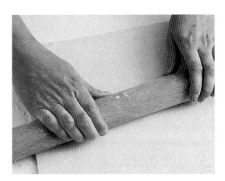

**4** Meanwhile, roll out the pastry until about 2cm/¾in larger all round than the top of the pie dish. Leave the pastry to relax while the chicken is cooling.

**5** Preheat the oven to 220°C/425°F/ Gas 7. Cut off a narrow strip around the edge of the pastry, then place the strip on the edge of the pie dish. Moisten the strip with a little water, then cover the dish with the pastry. Press the edges together to seal. Trim and neatly crimp the edge all round.

**6** Make a hole in the centre of the pastry and insert a small funnel of foil. Brush the pastry with beaten egg, then bake for 15–20 minutes.

**7** Reduce the oven temperature to 180°C/350°F/Gas 4. Mix the cream and eggs, then carefully pour into the pie through the funnel. Gently shake the pie dish to evenly distribute the cream mixture, then return the pie to the oven for a further 7 minutes. Let the pie cool for 5–10 minutes before serving warm, or serve it cold.

# GUINNESS AND OYSTER PIE

*BENEATH A CRUST OF CRISP YET FLAKY PUFF PASTRY, A TASTY, RICH STEW OF TENDER BEEF AND FRESH OYSTERS IS THE IDEAL ANTIDOTE TO WINTER CHILLS.*

## SERVES FOUR

### INGREDIENTS

450g/1lb stewing beef
30ml/2 tbsp plain (all-purpose) flour
15ml/1 tbsp vegetable oil
25g/1oz/2 tbsp butter
1 onion, sliced
150ml/¼ pint/⅔ cup Guinness
  (dark ale)
150ml/¼ pint/⅔ cup beef stock
5ml/1 tsp granulated sugar
bouquet garni
12 oysters, opened
350g/12oz puff pastry
1 egg, beaten
salt and ground black pepper
chopped fresh parsley, to garnish

**1** Preheat the oven to 180°C/350°F/ Gas 4. Trim any excess fat from the meat and cut it into 2.5cm/1in pieces. Place in a plastic bag with the flour and plenty of seasoning. Shake until the meat is well coated.

**2** Heat the oil and butter in a large flameproof casserole and fry the meat for 10 minutes until browned all over. Add the onion and continue cooking for 2–3 minutes until just softened. Pour in the Guinness and stock. Add the sugar and bouquet garni. Cover and cook in the oven for 1¼ hours.

**3** Remove the casserole from the oven, spoon the mixture into a large 2 litre/ 2 pint/5 cup pie dish and leave to cool for about 15 minutes. Increase the oven temperature to 200°C/400°F/Gas 6.

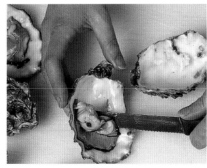

**4** Meanwhile, use a round-bladed knife to remove the oysters from their shells. Put them in a colander and rinse them well. Drain, then dry on kitchen paper. Stir into the beef mixture.

**5** Roll out the pastry until about 2cm/ ¾in larger than the top of the pie dish. Brush the edge of the dish with beaten egg and lay the pastry over the top. Trim neatly and decorate with leaves.

**6** Brush with the remaining egg and bake for 25 minutes until the pastry is puffed and golden. Serve at once, garnished with a little parsley.

**COOK'S TIP**
Use the pastry trimmings to make small decorations for the pie. To make leaves, cut the pastry into small diamond shapes and mark veins using the point of a small knife.

# STEAK AND KIDNEY PIE WITH MUSTARD GRAVY

*THIS IS A VARIATION OF A TRADITIONAL FAVOURITE. THE FRAGRANT MUSTARD, BAY AND PARSLEY GRAVY COMPLEMENTS THE BEEF BEAUTIFULLY.*

SERVES FOUR

INGREDIENTS
    450g/1lb puff pastry
    40ml/2½ tbsp plain
     (all-purpose) flour
    675g/1½lb rump (round)
     steak, cubed
    175g/6oz lamb's kidneys
    25g/1oz/2 tbsp butter
    1 onion, chopped
    15ml/1 tbsp English (hot) mustard
    2 bay leaves
    15ml/1 tbsp chopped fresh parsley
    150ml/¼ pint/⅔ cup beef stock
    1 egg, beaten
    salt and ground black pepper

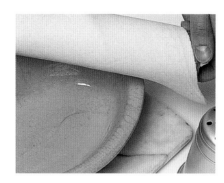

**1** Roll out two-thirds of the pastry on a floured surface to a thickness of 3mm/⅛in. Use to line the base and sides of a 1.5 litre/2½ pint/6¼ cup pie dish. Place a pie funnel in the centre of the dish.

**2** Put the flour, salt and pepper in a bowl and toss the steak in the mixture.

**3** Remove the fat, skin and tough central core from the kidneys, and slice them thickly. Add the slices to the steak and toss well.

**4** Melt the butter in a pan, add the onion and fry over a low heat, stirring occasionally, until soft and translucent. Add the mustard, bay leaves, parsley and stock and stir well.

**5** Preheat the oven to 190°C/375°F/ Gas 5. Place the steak and kidney in the pie dish and add the stock mixture.

**6** Roll out the remaining puff pastry to a thickness of 3mm/⅛in to use for the pie lid. Brush the edges of the pastry case with beaten egg and cover with the lid. Press the edges firmly together to seal, then trim. Use the trimmings to decorate the top with pastry leaves.

**7** Brush the pie with a little beaten egg and make a small hole in the pastry lid for the funnel. Bake for about 1 hour until the pastry is well risen and golden brown. Serve the pie hot, straight from the pie dish.

**COOK'S TIP**
For an attractive appearance, scallop the pastry crust. Pressing down on the rim with the first two fingers of one hand, use the blunt side of a knife blade to draw the pastry towards the centre.

# TURKEY AND CRANBERRY PIE

*THE CRANBERRIES ADD A TART LAYER TO THIS MEATY PIE. CRANBERRY SAUCE CAN BE USED IF FRESH CRANBERRIES ARE NOT AVAILABLE. THE PIE FREEZES WELL.*

## SERVES EIGHT

INGREDIENTS
  450g/1lb pork sausage meat (bulk pork sausage)
  450g/1lb lean minced (ground) pork
  15ml/1 tbsp ground coriander
  15ml/1 tbsp dried mixed herbs
  finely grated rind of 2 large oranges
  10ml/2 tsp grated fresh root ginger or 2.5ml/½ tsp ground ginger
  10ml/2 tsp salt
  450g/1lb turkey breast fillets
  115g/4oz/1 cup fresh cranberries
  ground black pepper
  1 egg, beaten
  300ml/½ pint/1¼ cups aspic jelly, made according to the instructions on the packet
For the hot water crust pastry
  450g/1lb/4 cups plain (all-purpose) flour
  5ml/1 tsp salt
  150g/5oz/⅔ cup lard
  150ml/¼ pint/⅔ cup mixed milk and water

**1** Preheat the oven to 180°C/350°F/ Gas 4. Place a baking sheet in the oven to preheat. In a bowl, mix together the sausage meat, pork, coriander, herbs, orange rind, ginger and salt. Season with black pepper to taste.

**2** To make the pastry, sift the flour into a large bowl with the salt. Heat the lard in a small pan with the milk and water until just beginning to boil. Remove the pan from the heat and allow the mixture to cool slightly.

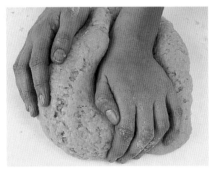

**3** Quickly stir the liquid into the flour until a very stiff dough is formed. Place on a clean work surface and knead until smooth. Cut one-third off the dough for the lid, wrap in clear film (plastic wrap) and keep in a warm place.

**4** Roll out the large piece of dough on a floured surface and use to line the base and sides of a greased 20cm/8in loose-based, springform cake tin. Work with the dough while it is still warm, as it will break if it becomes too cold.

**5** Thinly slice the turkey breast fillets. Put them between two pieces of clear film and flatten with a rolling pin to a thickness of 3mm/⅛in. Spoon half the pork mixture into the tin, pressing it well into the edges. Cover it with half the turkey slices and then the cranberries, followed by the remaining turkey and finally the rest of the pork mixture.

**6** Roll out the remaining dough and use to cover the filling, trimming off any excess and sealing the edges with a little beaten egg. Make a steam hole in the centre of the lid and decorate the top by cutting pastry trimmings into leaf shapes. Brush with some beaten egg and bake for 2 hours. Cover the pie with foil if the top gets too brown.

**7** Place the pie on a wire rack to cool. When cold, use a funnel to fill the pie with liquid aspic jelly. Leave the jelly to set for a few hours or overnight, before unmoulding the pie to serve it.

# BACON AND EGG PIE

*WHOLE EGGS ARE BROKEN OVER SMOKED BACON AND SOFTENED ONIONS BEFORE BEING COVERED IN PASTRY IN A DOUBLE-CRUST PIE, IN THIS CELEBRATION OF THE BEST OF BREAKFAST INGREDIENTS.*

SERVES FOUR

INGREDIENTS
    30ml/2 tbsp sunflower oil
    4 smoked bacon rashers (strips), cut
        into 4cm/1½in pieces
    1 small onion, finely chopped
    5 eggs
    25ml/1½ tbsp chopped fresh parsley
    salt and ground black pepper
    a little milk, to glaze
For the shortcrust pastry
    350g/12oz/3 cups plain
        (all-purpose) flour
    pinch of salt
    115g/4oz/½ cup butter, diced
    50g/2oz/¼ cup lard or white
        vegetable fat
    75–90ml/5–6 tbsp chilled water

**1** To make the pastry, sift the flour and salt into a large bowl and rub or cut in the fat until the mixture resembles fine breadcrumbs. Sprinkle over most of the water and mix to a pliable dough, adding more water if required. Knead until smooth, then wrap in clear film (plastic wrap) and chill for 30 minutes.

**2** Butter a deep 20cm/8in flan tin (quiche pan). Roll out two-thirds of the pastry and use to line the flan tin. Cover the pastry case. Chill for 30 minutes.

**3** Preheat the oven to 200°C/400°F/ Gas 6. Heat the oil in a pan, add the bacon and cook for a few minutes, then add the onion and cook until soft. Drain on kitchen paper and leave to cool.

**4** Cover the base of the pastry case with the bacon mixture, spreading it evenly, then break the eggs on to the bacon, spacing them evenly apart. Carefully tilt the flan tin so the egg whites flow together. Sprinkle the eggs with the chopped parsley, a little salt and plenty of black pepper. Place a baking sheet in the oven to heat.

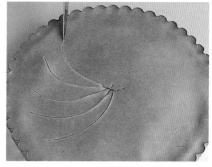

**5** Roll out the remaining pastry, dampen the edges and place over the pie. Roll over the top with a rolling pin to seal the edge and remove the excess pastry. With a sharp knife, carefully cut curved lines from the centre of the lid to within 2cm/¾in of the edge. Lightly brush the pie with the milk to glaze.

**6** Place the pie on the hot baking sheet and bake for 10 minutes, then lower the oven temperature to 180°C/350°F/Gas 4 and bake for a further 20 minutes. Leave to cool for a few minutes before cutting and serving.

# CHEESE AND SPINACH FLAN

*THE DECORATIVE PASTRY TOPPING FOR THIS FLAN IS MADE USING A LATTICE CUTTER. IF YOU DON'T HAVE ONE, CUT THE PASTRY INTO FINE STRIPS AND WEAVE THEM INTO A LATTICE.*

### SERVES EIGHT

INGREDIENTS
  450g/1lb frozen spinach
  1 onion, chopped
  pinch of grated nutmeg
  225g/8oz/1 cup cottage cheese
  2 large eggs
  50g/2oz Parmesan cheese, grated
  150ml/¼ pint/⅔ cup single
    (light) cream
  1 egg, beaten
  salt and ground black pepper
For the cheese pastry
  225g/8oz/2 cups plain
    (all-purpose) flour
  115g/4oz/½ cup butter
  2.5ml/½ tsp English (hot) mustard
  2.5ml/½ tsp paprika
  115g/4oz Cheddar cheese,
    finely grated
  45–60ml/3–4 tbsp chilled water

**1** To make the pastry, sift the flour into a large mixing bowl and rub or cut in the butter until the mixture resembles fine breadcrumbs. Stir in the mustard powder, paprika, salt and cheese. Bind to a soft, pliable dough with the chilled water. Knead lightly until smooth, wrap in clear film (plastic wrap) and chill for 30 minutes.

**2** Put the spinach and onion in a pan, and cook until the onion has softened. Increase the heat to evaporate any liquid in the pan. Season with salt, pepper and nutmeg. Put the mixture into a bowl and add the cottage cheese, eggs, Parmesan and cream. Mix well.

**3** Preheat the oven to 200°C/400°F/ Gas 6. Put a baking sheet in the oven to preheat. Roll out two-thirds of the pastry on a lightly floured surface and use to line a 23cm/9in loose-based flan tin (quiche pan). Press the pastry into the edges and make a narrow lip around the top edge. Remove the excess pastry with a rolling pin. Spoon the filling into the flan case.

**4** Roll out the remaining pastry and cut it with a lattice pastry cutter. Carefully open the lattice and, with the help of a rolling pin, lay it over the flan. Lightly brush the edges with beaten egg, press together and trim off the excess pastry. Brush the top of the pastry lattice with beaten egg and bake on the hot baking sheet for 35–40 minutes, or until golden brown. Serve hot or cold.

# POTATO AND LEEK FILO PIE

*THIS FILO PASTRY WOULD MAKE AN ATTRACTIVE AND UNUSUAL CENTREPIECE FOR A VEGETARIAN BUFFET. THIS PIE IS BEST SERVED COLD, WITH A SELECTION OF SALADS.*

SERVES EIGHT

INGREDIENTS
  800g/1¾lb new potatoes
  2 large leeks
  75g/3oz/6 tbsp butter
  15g/½oz/½ cup fresh parsley,
    finely chopped
  60ml/4 tbsp chopped mixed
    fresh herbs
  12 sheets of filo pastry, thawed
    if frozen
  150g/5oz Cheshire or Lancashire
    cheese, sliced
  2 garlic cloves, finely chopped
  250ml/8fl oz/1 cup double
    (heavy) cream
  2 large egg yolks
  salt and ground black pepper

**1** Preheat the oven to 190°C/375°F/Gas 5. Slice the potatoes and cook them in a pan of salted boiling water for 3–4 minutes, then drain and set aside.

**2** Trim the leeks and rinse thoroughly under cold running water. Drain them well, then slice thinly.

**3** Melt 25g/1oz/2 tbsp of the butter in a frying pan, add the sliced leeks and fry, stirring occasionally, until softened. Remove from the heat, season with pepper and stir in half the parsley and half the mixed herbs. Set the pan aside.

**4** Melt the remaining butter in a pan. Line a deep 23cm/9in loose-based cake tin with 6–7 sheets of filo pastry, lightly brushing each layer with butter. Let the edges of the pastry overhang the tin.

**5** Layer the potatoes, leek mixture and cheese in the tin, sprinkling some of the herbs and all the garlic between each of the layers. Season each with salt and plenty of pepper.

**COOK'S TIPS**
• Any fresh herbs can be used for this pie, but chervil, chives, tarragon and basil work particularly well. Chop them with a mezzaluna or cook's knife just before adding them to the pie.
• Most moist, crumbly, richly-flavoured cheeses will work well in this dish, such as Stilton, Cheddar and Milawa Blue.

**6** Fold the overhanging pastry over the filling and cover with 2 sheets of filo, tucking in the sides to fit. Brush with melted butter. Cover the pie loosely with foil and bake for 35 minutes. (Keep the remaining sheets of filo pastry covered with clear film (plastic wrap) and a damp dishtowel.)

**7** Meanwhile, in a small bowl, beat the cream, egg yolks and remaining herbs together. Remove the foil from the pie, make a hole in the centre of the pastry and gradually pour in the egg and cream mixture.

**8** Lower the oven temperature to 180°C/350°F/Gas 4. Cut the remaining pastry into strips and arrange them on top of the pie, gently teasing the strips into decorative loose swirls and folds, then brush the top of the pie with melted butter.

**9** Bake the pie for 25–30 minutes more until the top is golden and crisp. Allow the pie to cool before transferring it to a large platter and serving.

# SPINACH FILO PIE

*THIS POPULAR SPINACH AND FILO PASTRY PIE IS SOMETIMES CALLED SPANAKOPITA IN ITS NATIVE GREECE. THERE ARE SEVERAL WAYS OF MAKING IT, BUT FETA IS INEVITABLY INCLUDED.*

SERVES SIX

INGREDIENTS

1kg/2¼lb fresh spinach
4 spring onions (scallions), chopped
300g/11oz feta cheese, crumbled or
   coarsely grated
2 large eggs, beaten
30ml/2 tbsp chopped fresh parsley
15ml/1 tbsp chopped fresh dill
45ml/3 tbsp currants (optional)
about 8 sheets of filo pastry, each
   measuring 30 × 18cm/12 × 7in
150ml/¼ pint/⅔ cup olive oil
ground black pepper

**VARIATION**
Any crumbly hard cheese will work well in this pie. Try English Lancashire or Vermont Cheddar for a change.

**1** Break off any thick stalks from the spinach, then blanch the leaves in a very small amount of boiling water for 1–2 minutes until just wilted.

**2** Drain and refresh under cold water. Drain again, squeeze the spinach dry and chop it roughly.

**3** Place the spinach in a bowl with the spring onions and cheese, then pour in the eggs and stir them in thoroughly. Mix in the herbs and currants, if using. Season with pepper.

**4** Preheat the oven to 190°C/375°F/ Gas 5. Brush a sheet of filo with oil and fit it into a 23cm/9in pie dish, allowing it to hang over the edges. Add 3–4 more sheets, placing them at different angles and brushing each with oil.

**5** Spoon the filling into the filo pastry case, then top with all but one of the remaining filo sheets, brushing each filo sheet with oil as you go. Fold the overhanging filo pastry over the top sheets to seal. Brush the reserved filo with oil and scrunch it over the top of the pie.

**6** Brush the pie with oil. Sprinkle with a little water to stop the filo edges from curling, then place on a baking sheet. Bake for about 40 minutes until golden and crisp. Allow the pie to cool for 15 minutes before serving.

# CHICKEN AND APRICOT FILO PIE

*THE FILLING FOR THIS UNUSUAL YET UTTERLY DELICIOUS PIE HAS A MIDDLE EASTERN FLAVOUR — CHICKEN COMBINED WITH APRICOTS, BULGUR WHEAT, NUTS AND SPICES.*

SERVES SIX

INGREDIENTS
  75g/3oz/½ cup bulgur wheat
  75g/3oz/6 tbsp butter
  1 onion, chopped
  450g/1lb minced (ground) chicken
  50g/2oz/¼ cup ready-to-eat dried
    apricots, finely chopped
  25g/1oz/¼ cup chopped almonds
  5ml/1 tsp ground cinnamon
  2.5ml/½ tsp ground allspice
  60ml/4 tbsp Greek (US strained
    plain) yogurt
  15ml/1 tbsp chopped fresh chives
  30ml/2 tbsp chopped fresh parsley
  8 large sheets of filo pastry
  salt and ground black pepper
  chives, to garnish

**1** Soak the bulgur wheat in 120ml/
4fl oz/½ cup boiling water for about
10 minutes until the water is absorbed.

**2** Heat 25g/1oz/2 tbsp of the butter in
a frying pan, add the onion and chicken
and gently fry until golden.

**3** Stir in the apricots, almonds and
bulgur wheat and cook for 2 minutes.
Remove from the heat and stir in the
cinnamon, allspice, yogurt, chives and
parsley. Season with salt and pepper.

**4** Preheat the oven to 200°C/ 400°F/
Gas 6. Melt the remaining butter. Unroll
the filo pastry and cut into 25cm/10in
rounds. Keep the pastry rounds covered
with a damp dishtowel to prevent them
from drying out.

**5** Line a 23cm/9in loose-based flan tin
(quiche pan) with three filo rounds,
brushing each one with butter as you
go. Spoon in the chicken mixture and
cover with three more rounds, brushing
with melted butter as before.

**COOK'S TIP**
Thaw frozen filo pastry well before use,
following the instructions on the packet.

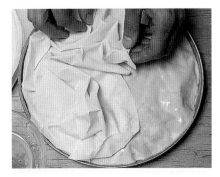

**6** Crumple the remaining two pastry
rounds and place them on top of the
pie, then brush over the remaining
melted butter. Bake the pie for about
30 minutes until the pastry is golden
brown and crisp. Serve the pie hot or
cold, cut in wedges and garnished with
a few chives.

# SAVOURY PARCELS AND PASTRY CASES

*You'll find all manner of traditional parcels and pastry cases here and some a little out of the ordinary. Pastry is amazingly versatile and can be wrapped around large or small joints of meat, used to enclose a rich mixture of wild game, or cut and braided. Some such as Beef Wellington or Mediterranean One-crust Pie are blissfully simple, but still look and taste wonderful. Try Chicken and Couscous Parcels for a light lunch or Fillets of Sea Bream in Filo Pastry for a dinner party to remember.*

# LAMB PIE WITH PEAR AND MINT SAUCE

*COOKING LAMB WITH FRUIT IS AN IDEA DERIVED FROM TRADITIONAL PERSIAN CUISINE. THE GINGER AND MINT ADD A DELIGHTFUL BITE TO THE MILD FLAVOURS IN THIS DISH.*

SERVES SIX

INGREDIENTS
400g/14oz can pear halves
  in juice
50g/2oz/¼ cup butter
1 small onion, chopped
grated rind of 1 lemon
75g/3oz/1 cup coarse wholemeal
  (whole-wheat) breadcrumbs
1.5ml/¼ tsp ground ginger
1 small egg, beaten
900g/2lb boned and rolled loin
  of lamb
8 large sheets of filo pastry
10ml/2 tsp finely chopped fresh mint
  plus a few mint sprigs, to garnish
salt and ground black pepper

**1** Preheat the oven to 180°C/350°F/ Gas 4. Drain the pears, reserving the juice. Set half the pears aside and chop the remainder.

**2** Melt 15g/½oz/1 tbsp of the butter in a pan and add the onion. Cook until soft. Put in a bowl and add the lemon rind, breadcrumbs, chopped pears and ginger. Bind with egg and season well.

**3** Open out the lamb, fat side down, and season. Place the pear stuffing along the middle of the lamb and roll the meat around it. Secure with skewers while you tie it up with string (twine).

**4** Heat a roasting pan in the oven and brown the loin of lamb slowly on all sides. This will take 20–30 minutes. Remove from the oven, leave to cool, then chill until needed.

**5** Increase the oven temperature to 200°C/400°F/Gas 6. Melt the remaining butter. Brush two sheets of filo pastry with melted butter. Overlap the sheets of filo to make a square. Place the next two sheets on top and brush with butter. Continue until all the pastry has been used.

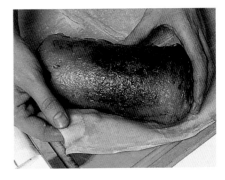

**6** Place the roll of lamb diagonally across one corner of the pastry. Fold the corner over the lamb, fold in the sides, and brush the pastry well with melted butter. Roll up the lamb in the pastry, tucking in the edges as you go.

**7** Place the filo-wrapped lamb, seam side down, on a buttered baking sheet and brush it all over with the remaining melted butter. Bake the lamb for about 30 minutes, or until the pastry is crisp and golden brown.

**8** To make the sauce, process the reserved pears with their juice and the mint in a food processor or blender. Spoon the pear and mint sauce into a small bowl and serve with the lamb, garnished with a few mint sprigs.

# BEEF WELLINGTON

*THIS DISH, A FILLET OF BEEF BAKED IN PUFF PASTRY, IS A VARIATION OF THE CLASSIC FRENCH BOEUF EN CROÛTE. THE ENGLISH NAME WAS APPLIED IN 1815 IN HONOUR OF THE DUKE OF WELLINGTON.*

SERVES SIX

INGREDIENTS
1.6kg/3¼lb fillet (tenderloin) of beef
45ml/3 tbsp sunflower oil
115g/4oz/1½ cups button (white)
  mushrooms, chopped
2 garlic cloves, crushed
175g/6oz smooth liver pâté
30ml/2 tbsp chopped fresh parsley
400g/14oz puff pastry
1 egg, beaten
salt and ground black pepper

1 Preheat the oven to 220°C/425°F/ Gas 7. Tie the beef with string (twine). Heat 30ml/2 tbsp of the oil in a frying pan, and brown the beef on all sides for 10 minutes. Put in a roasting pan and roast for 20 minutes. Remove and set aside to cool. Leave the oven on.

2 Heat the remaining oil in a frying pan and cook the mushrooms and garlic for about 5 minutes until softened. Beat the mushroom mixture into the pâté with the chopped parsley, and season well. Set aside to cool.

3 Roll out the puff pastry into a sheet large enough to enclose the beef, plus a strip to spare. Trim off the spare pastry. Spread the pâté mixture down the middle of the pastry. Untie the beef and lay it on top of the pâté mixture.

4 Brush the edges of the pastry with beaten egg and fold the pastry over the meat to enclose it in a neat parcel. Seal the edges well. Place the meat parcel on a baking sheet, seam side down. Cut decorative leaf shapes from the reserved pastry. Brush the parcel with beaten egg, decorate with the pastry leaves and brush with egg. Chill for about 10 minutes.

5 Bake the beef for 50–60 minutes, covering it loosely with foil after about 30 minutes to prevent the pastry from over-browning. Transfer to a serving platter and leave to stand for about 10 minutes. Serve in thick slices, and garnish each portion with parsley.

# RICH GAME PIE

*TERRIFIC FOR STYLISH PICNICS OR JUST AS SMART FOR A MORE FORMAL SPECIAL OCCASION, THIS PIE LOOKS SPECTACULAR WHEN BAKED IN A FLUTED RAISED PIE MOULD.*

SERVES TEN

INGREDIENTS
    25g/1oz/2 tbsp butter
    1 onion, finely chopped
    2 garlic cloves, finely chopped
    900g/2lb mixed boneless game meat,
        such as skinless pheasant and/or
        pigeon breast, venison and
        rabbit, diced
    30ml/2 tbsp chopped mixed
        fresh herbs
    1 egg, beaten
    salt and ground black pepper
For the pâté
    50g/2oz/¼ cup butter
    2 garlic cloves, finely chopped
    450g/1lb chicken livers, trimmed
        and chopped
    60ml/4 tbsp brandy
    5ml/1 tsp ground mace
For the hot water crust pastry
    675g/1½lb/6 cups strong white
        bread flour
    5ml/1 tsp salt
    120ml/4fl oz/½ cup milk
    90ml/3fl oz/6 tbsp water
    115g/4oz/½ cup lard, diced
    115g/4oz/½ cup butter, diced
For the jelly
    300ml/½ pint/1¼ cups game or
        beef consommé
    2.5ml/½ tsp powdered gelatine

**1** Melt the butter in a small pan, then add the onion and garlic, and cook gently until softened but not coloured. Remove the pan from the heat and add the onions and garlic to the diced game meat and the chopped mixed herbs. Mix well. Season with salt and plenty of pepper, cover and chill.

**2** To make the pâté, melt the butter in a frying pan, add the garlic and chicken livers and cook over a medium heat, stirring frequently, until just browned. Remove the pan from the heat and stir in the brandy and ground mace. Purée the mixture in a blender or food processor until smooth, then set aside and leave to cool.

**3** To make the pastry, sift the flour and salt into a bowl and make a well in the centre. Pour the milk and water into a pan. Add the lard and butter and heat gently until melted, then bring to the boil. Immediately, pour the hot liquid into the well in the flour and beat until smooth. Cover and leave until cool enough to handle.

**4** Preheat the oven to 200°C/400°F/ Gas 6. Roll out two-thirds of the pastry and use to line a 23cm/9in raised pie mould. Spoon in half the game mixture and press it down evenly. Add the pâté and then top with the remaining game.

**5** Roll out the remaining pastry to form a lid. Brush the edge of the pastry case with a little water and cover with the pastry lid. Trim off the excess pastry from around the edge. Pinch the edges together to seal in the filling. Make two holes in the centre of the lid and brush the lid with beaten egg. Use the pastry trimmings to make small leaves to decorate the pie. Brush the leaves with a little beaten egg.

**6** Bake the pie for 20 minutes, then cover with foil and cook for 10 minutes more. Reduce the oven temperature to 150°C/300°F/Gas 2. Lightly glaze the pie again with beaten egg and cook for a further 1½ hours, keeping the top covered loosely with foil.

**7** Remove the pie from the oven and leave it to stand for 15 minutes to cool slightly. Increase the oven temperature to 200°C/400°F/Gas 6. Stand the tin on a baking sheet and remove the sides. Quickly glaze the sides of the pie with beaten egg and cover the top with foil. Cook the pie for a final 15 minutes to brown the sides. Leave the pie to cool completely, then chill overnight.

**8** Next day, make the jelly. Heat the game or beef consommé in a small pan until just beginning to bubble, whisk in the gelatine until dissolved and leave to cool until just setting. Using a small funnel, carefully pour the jellied consommé into the holes in the pie. Chill until set. This pie will keep in the refrigerator for up to three days.

# FILLETS OF SEA BREAM IN FILO PASTRY

*ANY FIRM FISH FILLETS CAN BE USED FOR THIS DISH. EACH LITTLE PARCEL IS A MEAL IN ITSELF AND CAN BE PREPARED SEVERAL HOURS IN ADVANCE, WHICH MAKES THIS IDEAL FOR ENTERTAINING.*

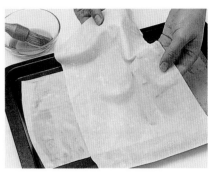

**2** Thinly slice the potatoes lengthways. Brush a baking tray with a little oil. Lay a sheet of filo pastry on the tray, brush it with oil, then lay a second sheet crossways over the first. Repeat with two more sheets. Arrange a quarter of the sliced potatoes in the centre of the pastry, season well and add a quarter of the shredded sorrel. Lay a bream fillet on top, skin-side up. Season again.

**3** Loosely fold the filo pastry up and over to make a neat parcel. Make three more parcels in the same way. Place on the baking tray and brush them with half the butter. Bake for 20 minutes until the filo has fully puffed up and is golden brown.

SERVES FOUR

INGREDIENTS
  8 small waxy salad potatoes
  200g/7oz sorrel, stalks removed
  30ml/2 tbsp olive oil
  16 sheets of filo pastry, thawed
    if frozen
  4 sea bream fillets, about 175g/6oz
    each, scaled but not skinned
  50g/2oz/¼ cup butter, melted
  120ml/4fl oz/½ cup fish stock
  250ml/8fl oz/1 cup double
    (heavy) cream
  salt and ground black pepper
  finely diced red (bell) pepper,
    to garnish

**VARIATION**
Use small spinach leaves or baby chard in place of the sorrel.

**1** Preheat the oven to 200°C/400°F/ Gas 6. Cook the salad potatoes in lightly salted boiling water for 15–20 minutes, until just tender. Drain and set aside to cool. Shred half the sorrel leaves by piling up six or eight at a time, rolling them up like a fat cigar and slicing them with a sharp knife. Reserve the rest of the sorrel.

**4** Meanwhile, make the sorrel sauce. Heat the remaining butter in a small pan, add the reserved sorrel and cook until it wilts. Stir in the fish stock and cream. Heat almost to boiling point, stirring constantly. Season and keep hot. Serve the fish parcels garnished with red pepper and offer the sauce separately, in its own bowl.

# CHICKEN AND COUSCOUS PARCELS

*BASED ON THE TURKISH BÖREK OR BOREG, THESE SAVOURY RICH PASTRY PARCELS ARE SERVED AT ROOM TEMPERATURE WITH A YOGURT SAUCE, SPIKED WITH CAYENNE AND COOLED WITH MINT.*

SERVES FOUR

INGREDIENTS
    50g/2oz/⅓ cup couscous
    45ml/3 tbsp olive oil
    1 onion, chopped
    115g/4oz/1½ cups mushrooms
    1 garlic clove, crushed
    115g/4oz cooked chicken, diced
      (about 1 cup)
    30ml/2 tbsp walnuts, chopped
    30ml/2 tbsp raisins
    60ml/4 tbsp chopped fresh parsley
    5ml/1 tsp chopped fresh thyme
    2 eggs, hard-boiled and peeled
    salt and ground black pepper
For the pastry
    400g/14oz/3½ cups self-raising
      (self-rising) flour
    1 egg, plus extra for glazing
    150ml/¼ pint/⅔ cup natural
      (plain) yogurt
    150ml/¼ pint/⅔ cup olive oil
    grated rind of ½ lemon
For the yogurt sauce
    200ml/7fl oz/scant 1 cup natural
      (plain) yogurt
    45ml/3 tbsp chopped fresh mint
    2.5ml/½ tsp caster (superfine) sugar
    1.5ml/¼ tsp cayenne pepper
    1.5ml/¼ tsp celery salt
    a little milk or water (optional)

**1** Preheat the oven to 190°C/375°F/ Gas 5. Place the couscous in a bowl and just cover with boiling water. Soak for 10 minutes, or until all the liquid has been absorbed.

**2** Heat the oil in a frying pan, add the onion and cook over a medium heat until soft but without letting it colour. Add the mushrooms and garlic, and cook until the juices begin to run. Increase the heat to evaporate the juices.

**VARIATION**
Alternative fillings for these parcels include mixed cheeses and herbs; mushrooms with ground cumin and coriander; or a spicy potato and vegetable mixture.

**3** Transfer the mushroom and onion mixture to a large mixing bowl, add the chicken, walnuts, raisins, parsley, thyme and couscous, and stir well. Chop the eggs roughly and stir them into the mixture with seasoning to taste.

**4** To make the pastry, sift the flour and 5ml/1 tsp salt into a bowl. Make a well in the centre, add the egg, yogurt, olive oil and lemon rind, and mix together with a round-bladed knife.

**5** On a floured surface, roll out the pastry to a 30cm/12in round. Pile the filling into the centre and bring the edges over to enclose the filling. Place seam side down on a baking sheet and gently flatten with your hand. Glaze with beaten egg and bake for 25 minutes.

**6** Meanwhile, make the sauce. Mix together all the ingredients, adding milk or water if the mixture is too thick. Spoon a little sauce over each serving.

# CHICKEN, CHEESE AND LEEK PARCEL

*STRIPS OF PUFF PASTRY ARE CLEVERLY CROSSED OVER A CREAMY CHICKEN FILLING TO MAKE THIS*
*ATTRACTIVE FAMILY-SIZE PIE, WHICH TASTES GOOD EITHER WARM OR COLD.*

SERVES SIX

INGREDIENTS
    1 roast chicken, about 1.6kg/3½lb
    40g/1½oz/3 tbsp butter
    2 large leeks, thinly sliced
    2 garlic cloves, crushed
    115g/4oz/1 cup button (white)
      mushrooms, sliced
    200g/7oz/scant 1 cup low-fat
      cream cheese
    grated rind of 1 small lemon
    45ml/3 tbsp chopped fresh flat
      leaf parsley
    500g/1¼lb puff pastry
    1 egg, beaten
    salt and ground black pepper
    fresh herbs, to garnish

**1** Strip the meat from the chicken, discarding the skin and bones. Chop or shred the meat and set it aside.

**2** Melt the butter in a pan, add the leeks and garlic and cook for 10 minutes. Stir in the mushrooms and cook for 5 minutes. Leave to cool, then add the cream cheese, lemon rind, parsley and seasoning. Stir in the chicken.

**VARIATION**
For a richer flavour, use dolcelatte cheese instead of the cream cheese.

**3** Roll out the pastry on a lightly floured work surface to a large rectangle, about 35 × 25cm/14 × 10in. Using a rolling pin to help you, lift the pastry on to a non-stick baking sheet.

**4** Spoon the filling on to the pastry, leaving a generous margin at each end, and about 10cm/4in on each long side. Use a sharp knife to cut the pastry sides diagonally in strips, cutting up to the filling at 2cm/¾in intervals.

**5** Brush the edges of the pastry with a little of the beaten egg. Cross the pastry strips over each other alternately to enclose the filling. Seal the edges.

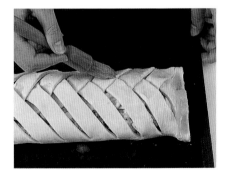

**6** Glaze the top with beaten egg. Leave the pie to rest while you preheat the oven to 200°C/400°F/Gas 6. Bake for about 15 minutes, then lower the oven temperature to 190°C/375°F/Gas 5 and bake for a further 15 minutes, or until the pastry is golden brown and crisp. Allow to stand for 10 minutes before sliding the parcel on to a board or platter to serve. Garnish with herbs.

# MUSHROOM, NUT AND PRUNE JALOUSIE

*JALOUSIE, THE FRENCH WORD FOR SHUTTER, REFERS TO THIS PIE'S SLATTED TOP. IT HAS A RICH NUTTY FILLING THAT WILL BE ENJOYED BY VEGETARIANS AND MEAT-EATERS ALIKE.*

SERVES SIX

INGREDIENTS
75g/3oz/⅓ cup green lentils, rinsed
5ml/1 tsp vegetable bouillon powder
15ml/1 tbsp sunflower oil
2 large leeks, sliced
2 garlic cloves, chopped
200g/7oz/3 cups field (portabello) mushrooms, finely chopped
10ml/2 tsp dried mixed herbs
75g/3oz/¾ cup chopped mixed nuts
15ml/1 tbsp pine nuts
75g/3oz/⅓ cup ready-to-eat pitted prunes
25g/1oz/½ cup fresh breadcrumbs
2 eggs, beaten
500g/1¼lb puff pastry
salt and ground black pepper

**1** Put the lentils in a pan and cover with cold water. Bring to the boil, then reduce the heat slightly and stir in the vegetable bouillon powder. Partly cover the pan and simmer for 20 minutes or until the lentils are tender and have absorbed the liquid. Set aside.

**2** Heat the oil in a large heavy frying pan, add the leeks and garlic and fry for about 5 minutes, or until just softened. Add the mushrooms and herbs and cook for a further 5 minutes.

**3** Transfer the leek and mushroom mixture to a mixing bowl using a slotted spoon. Stir in the chopped nuts, pine nuts, prunes, fresh breadcrumbs and lentils. Preheat the oven to 220°C/425°F/Gas 7.

**4** Add two-thirds of the beaten egg to the mushroom mixture and season well. Set aside and leave to cool.

**5** Meanwhile, roll out just under half the pastry to a 25 × 15cm/10 × 6in rectangle, then lay it on a dampened baking sheet. Roll out the remaining pastry to a 28 × 19cm/11 × 7½in rectangle, dust it with flour, then fold in half lengthways. Make a series of cuts across the fold, 1cm/½in apart, leaving a 2.5cm/1in border around the edge.

**6** Spoon the mushroom mixture evenly over the pastry base, leaving a 2.5cm/1in border. Dampen the edges of the pastry with water. Open out the folded piece of pastry and carefully lay it over the filling. Press the edges of the pastry together to seal, trim off the excess then crimp the edges.

**7** Brush the top of the pastry with the remaining beaten egg and bake for 25–30 minutes until golden. Leave to cool slightly before serving.

# MEDITERRANEAN ONE-CRUST PIE

*THIS FREE-FORM PIE ENCASES A RICH TOMATO, AUBERGINE AND KIDNEY BEAN FILLING. IF YOUR PASTRY CRACKS, JUST PATCH IT UP — A ROUGH APPEARANCE ADDS TO THE PIE'S RUSTIC CHARACTER.*

SERVES FOUR

INGREDIENTS

500g/1¼ 1b aubergine
  (eggplant), cubed
1 red (bell) pepper
30ml/2 tbsp olive oil
1 large onion, finely chopped
1 courgette (zucchini), sliced
2 garlic cloves, crushed
15ml/1 tbsp chopped fresh oregano
  or 5ml/1 tsp dried, plus extra fresh
  oregano to garnish
200g/7oz can red kidney beans,
  drained and rinsed
115g/4oz/1 cup pitted black
  olives, rinsed
150ml/¼ pint/⅔ cup passata (bottled
  strained tomatoes)
1 egg, beaten, or a little milk
30ml/2 tbsp semolina
salt and ground black pepper
For the cheese pastry
  75g/3oz/⅔ cup plain
    (all-purpose) flour
  75g/3oz/⅔ cup wholemeal
    (whole-wheat) flour
  75g/3oz/6 tbsp vegetable margarine
  50g/2oz/⅔ cup freshly grated
    Parmesan cheese
  60–90ml/4–6 tbsp chilled water

**1** Preheat the oven to 220°C/425°F/ Gas 7. To make the pastry, sift both the flours into a bowl, tipping the bran into the bowl. Rub or cut in the margarine until the mixture resembles breadcrumbs, then stir in the Parmesan. Mix in just enough chilled water to form a firm dough. Chill for 30 minutes.

**2** Transfer the dough to a lightly floured surface and knead into a smooth ball. Wrap in cling film (plastic wrap) and chill for 30 minutes.

**3** To make the filling, place the aubergine in a colander and sprinkle with salt, then leave for 30 minutes. Rinse and pat dry with kitchen paper. Meanwhile, place the red pepper on a baking sheet and roast in the oven for 20 minutes. Put the pepper in a plastic bag. When cool, remove, peel and seed, then dice the flesh. Set aside.

**4** Heat the oil in a large frying pan. Add the onion and fry for 5 minutes until softened and translucent, stirring occasionally. Add the aubergine and fry for 5 minutes until tender.

**5** Add the sliced courgettes, garlic and oregano, and cook for 5 minutes more, stirring often. Add the kidney beans and olives, stir well, then add the passata and season to taste with salt and black pepper. Cook until heated through, then set aside to cool.

**6** Roll out the pastry on a lightly floured surface to a rough 30cm/12in round. Place on a lightly oiled baking sheet. Brush with beaten egg or milk, sprinkle over the semolina, leaving a 4cm/1½in border, then spoon over the filling.

**7** Gather up the edges of the pastry to partly cover the filling – it should be open in the middle. Brush the pastry with the remaining egg or milk and bake for 30–35 minutes until golden.

# MUSHROOM AND QUAIL'S EGG GOUGÈRE

*GOUGÈRE IS A POPULAR PASTRY FROM THE BURGUNDY REGION OF FRANCE. IN THIS VERSION IT IS FILLED WITH WILD MUSHROOMS AND TINY, LIGHTLY BOILED QUAIL'S EGGS.*

SERVES FOUR TO SIX

INGREDIENTS

  25g/1oz/¼ cup cornflour (cornstarch)
  150ml/¼ pint/⅔ cup mixed red wine
    and water
  25g/1oz/2 tbsp butter
  1 onion, chopped
  2 celery sticks, sliced
  350g/12oz/4–5 cups mixed wild and
    cultivated mushrooms, halved
    or quartered
  150ml/¼ pint/⅔ cup stock
  dash of Worcestershire sauce
  15ml/1 tbsp chopped fresh parsley
  12 quail's eggs
For the choux pastry
  75g/3oz/6 tbsp butter, diced
  2.5ml/½ tsp salt
  175ml/6fl oz/¾ cup water
  100g/3¾oz/scant 1 cup plain
    (all-purpose) flour, sifted
  4 eggs
  115g/4oz/1 cup grated
    Gruyère cheese

**1** Preheat the oven to 220°F/425°C/ Gas 7. To make the pastry, melt the butter in a pan with the salt and water, and bring to the boil. Remove from the heat, add all the flour and beat with a wooden spoon until it forms a ball.

**2** Return the pan to the heat and cook, beating hard, for 1–2 minutes. Leave to cool slightly. Add two eggs, beating until the mixture becomes glossy. Beat in the third egg, then beat in as much of the fourth egg as you need to create glossy, soft pastry. Beat in half the cheese.

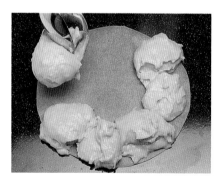

**3** Place a round of baking parchment on a large baking sheet and place large spoonfuls of the choux pastry evenly in a 20cm/8in circle. Position them close together so that they will join up as they cook. Bake the choux pastry for about 30 minutes until well risen and golden all over. Remove from the oven, cut a few slits in the side to release the steam and set aside to cool slightly.

**4** Mix the cornflour and wine and water in a bowl. Meanwhile, melt the butter in a pan, add the onion and celery and fry until soft. Add the mushrooms and cook gently, then add the wine mixture.

**5** Add the stock to the mushrooms and gradually stir in the cornflour mixture. Cook gently until it is starting to thicken. Add the Worcestershire sauce and parsley, and cook until thick.

**6** Place the quail's eggs in a pan of cold water, bring to the boil and cook for 1 minute. Cool thoroughly, then peel.

**7** To serve, slice the gougère in half horizontally. Fill with the mushroom mixture and top with the eggs. Replace the pastry lid, sprinkle over the remaining cheese and return to the oven until the cheese melts.

# SALMON IN PUFF PASTRY

*THIS FUN PARTY DISH HAS A VERY TASTY RICE, EGG AND SALMON FILLING, ENCASED IN AN ATTRACTIVE PUFF PASTRY CRUST. DON'T WORRY IF THE FISH SHAPE ISN'T PERFECT — THAT'S PART OF ITS APPEAL.*

SERVES SIX

INGREDIENTS
   450g/1lb puff pastry
   1 egg, beaten
   3 eggs, hard-boiled and peeled
   90ml/6 tbsp single (light) cream
   200g/7oz/1¾ cups cooked long grain
      white rice
   30ml/2 tbsp finely chopped
      fresh parsley
   10ml/2 tsp chopped
      fresh tarragon
   675g/1½lb fresh salmon fillets
   40g/1½oz/3 tbsp butter
   juice of ½ lemon
   salt and ground black pepper

**1** Preheat the oven to 190°C/375°F/ Gas 5. Roll out two-thirds of the pastry into a large oval, measuring 35cm/14in in length. Cut into a curved fish shape and place on a lightly greased large baking sheet.

**2** Use the trimmings to make narrow strips. Brush one side of each strip with a little beaten egg and secure in place around the rim of the pastry to make a raised edge.

**3** Prick the base all over with a fork, then bake for 8–10 minutes until the sides are well risen and the pastry is lightly golden. Leave to cool.

**4** Mash the hard-boiled eggs with the cream in a bowl, then stir in the cooked rice. Add the parsley and tarragon and season well. Spoon this mixture on to the prepared pastry.

**5** Cut the salmon into 2cm/¾in chunks. Melt the butter in a pan until it starts to sizzle, then add the salmon. Turn the pieces over in the butter so that they colour but do not cook through.

**6** Remove from the heat and arrange the salmon on top of the rice. Stir the lemon juice into the butter in the pan, then spoon the juices over the filling.

**7** Roll out the remaining pastry and cut out a rough semi-circle to cover the head portion and a tail shape to cover the tail. Brush both pieces of pastry with a little beaten egg and place on top of the fish, pressing the edges down firmly to secure. Score a criss-cross pattern on the tail.

**8** Cut the remaining pastry into small rounds and, starting from the tail end, arrange the rounds in overlapping lines to represent scales. Press the edges to seal. Add a smaller round for the eye. Brush the whole fish shape with the remaining beaten egg.

**9** Bake for 10 minutes, then lower the oven temperature to 160°C/325°F/Gas 3 and cook for a further 15–20 minutes until the pastry is golden all over. Slide on to a serving plate and serve.

**VARIATION**
If time is short, simply encase the salmon filling in a rectangular puff pastry parcel, scoring the top in a decorative criss-cross pattern.

# SPICY POTATO STRUDEL

*WRAP UP IN CRISP FILO PASTRY A TASTY MIXTURE OF VEGETABLES COOKED IN A SPICY, CREAMY SAUCE.*
*SERVE WITH A GOOD SELECTION OF CHUTNEYS OR A YOGURT AND MINT SAUCE.*

**2** Add the thyme, water and seasoning. Bring to the boil, then reduce the heat and simmer for 10 minutes until tender, stirring occasionally. Set aside to cool.

**3** Transfer the vegetable mixture to a large bowl, then mix in the egg, cream and cheese. Chill until you are ready to fill the filo pastry.

**4** Preheat the oven to 190°C/375°F/ Gas 5. Melt the remaining butter and lay out four sheets of filo pastry, slightly overlapping them to form a fairly large rectangle. Brush with some melted butter and fit the other sheets on top. Brush with some more of the butter.

**5** Spoon the filling along one long side of the pastry, then roll it up. Form it into a circle and place on a baking sheet. Brush with the remaining butter and sprinkle over the sesame seeds.

**6** Bake for about 25 minutes, or until golden and crisp. Leave the strudel to stand for 5 minutes before cutting into slices and serving.

## SERVES FOUR

### INGREDIENTS
65g/2½oz/5 tbsp butter
1 onion, chopped
2 carrots, coarsely grated
1 courgette (zucchini), chopped
350g/12oz firm potatoes, chopped
10ml/2 tsp mild curry paste
2.5ml/½ tsp dried thyme
150ml/¼ pint/⅔ cup water
1 egg, beaten
30ml/2 tbsp single (light) cream
50g/2oz/½ cup grated
  Cheddar cheese
8 sheets of filo pastry, thawed
  if frozen
sesame seeds, for sprinkling
salt and ground black pepper

**1** Melt 25g/1oz/2 tbsp of the butter in a frying pan and cook the onion, carrots, courgette and potatoes for 5 minutes, tossing them to ensure they cook evenly. Stir in the curry paste and continue to cook the vegetables for 1–2 minutes more until tender.

# SCALLOPS WITH WILD MUSHROOMS

*FROM THE DEPTHS OF THE SEA AND THE FOREST FLOOR COME TWO FLAVOURS THAT MARRY PERFECTLY IN A SMOOTH CREAMY SAUCE. CRISP PASTRY COMPLETES THE DISH.*

SERVES FOUR

INGREDIENTS
    350g/12oz puff pastry
    1 egg, beaten
    75g/3oz/6 tbsp butter
    12 scallops, trimmed and
        thickly sliced
    2 shallots, chopped
    ½ celery stick, cut into strips
    ½ carrot, cut into strips
    225g/8oz/3 cups assorted wild
        mushrooms, trimmed and sliced
    60ml/4 tbsp Noilly Prat or other
        dry vermouth
    150ml/¼ pint/⅔ cup crème fraîche
    4 egg yolks
    15ml/1 tbsp lemon juice
    salt, ground black pepper, celery salt
        and cayenne pepper

**1** Roll out the puff pastry on a floured surface, then cut out four 13cm/5in shell shapes, using a paper template if you need to. Mark a shell pattern on each with a small knife then brush with a little beaten egg. Place on a baking sheet, then chill for 1 hour. Preheat the oven to 200°C/400°F/Gas 6.

**2** Melt 25g/1oz/2 tbsp of the butter in a pan. Season the scallops with salt and black pepper, add them to the pan and cook for 30 seconds over a high heat. Transfer to a plate.

**3** Score an inner shell 2.5cm/1in from the outer edge of each pastry shape. Bake the shapes for 20–25 minutes until golden. Set aside on a wire rack.

**4** Fry the shallots, celery and carrot gently in the remaining butter. Add the mushrooms and cook until the juices begin to run. Pour in the vermouth and then increase the heat to evaporate the pan juices. Add the crème fraîche and cooked scallops and bring to a simmer (do not boil).

**5** Remove the pan from the heat and blend in the egg yolks. Return the pan to a gentle heat and cook for a moment or two until the sauce has thickened to the consistency of thin cream, then remove the pan from the heat. Season with celery salt and cayenne pepper, and add the lemon juice.

**6** Gently split the pastry shapes open and place the bases on four plates. Spoon in the filling and arrange the lids on top. Serve with potatoes and salad, if you like.

**COOK'S TIP**
Take care not to use dark mushrooms in a cream sauce as they will cause it to become an unattractive grey colour.

# SWEET PASTRIES AND TARTLETS

*This is a tantalizing collection of small sweet pastries to suit any occasion. Sweet and sticky Baklava and more substantial Poached Pear Tartlets with a rich and glossy chocolate sauce are perennial favourites, along with flavoured pastry doughs including lemon and coffee. Little pastries are found all around the world; try Gazelles' Horns with their orange-scented almond paste filling from Morocco or Baked Sweet Ravioli for true Italian style.*

# BAKED SWEET RAVIOLI

*THESE DELICIOUS SWEET RAVIOLI ARE MADE WITH A RICH PASTRY FLAVOURED WITH LEMON AND FILLED WITH A MIXTURE OF RICOTTA CHEESE, FRUIT AND CHOCOLATE.*

SERVES FOUR

INGREDIENTS
  175g/6oz/¾ cup ricotta cheese
  50g/2oz/¼ cup caster
    (superfine) sugar
  4ml/¾ tsp vanilla essence (extract)
  small egg, beaten, plus 1 egg yolk
  15ml/1 tbsp mixed candied fruits
  25g/1oz dark (bittersweet) chocolate,
    finely chopped
For the pastry
  225g/8oz/2 cups plain
    (all-purpose) flour
  65g/2½oz/⅓ cup caster
    (superfine) sugar
  90g/3½oz/scant ½ cup butter, diced
  1 egg
  5ml/1 tsp finely grated lemon rind

**1** To make the pastry, place the flour and sugar in a food processor and, with the motor running at full speed, slowly add the butter until fully worked into the mixture. Keep the motor running while you add the egg and lemon rind. The mixture should form a dough that just holds together.

**2** Transfer the dough to a sheet of clear film (plastic wrap), cover with another sheet of clear film and flatten into a round. Chill the pastry while you make the filling.

**3** Press the ricotta through a sieve into a mixing bowl. Stir in the sugar, vanilla essence, egg yolk, candied fruits and dark chocolate.

**4** Remove the pastry round from the refrigerator and allow it to come back to room temperature. Divide it in half and roll each half between sheets of clear film to make a rectangle measuring 15 × 56cm/6 × 22in. Preheat the oven to 180°C/350°F/Gas 4.

**5** Arrange heaped tablespoonfuls of the filling in two rows along one of the pastry strips, leaving a 2.5cm/1in margin around each. Brush the pastry between the mounds of filling with beaten egg. Place the second strip of pastry on top and press down between each mound of filling to seal.

**6** Use a 6cm/2½in plain pastry cutter to cut around each mound of filling to make small circular ravioli. Gently pinch each ravioli with your fingertips to seal the edges.

**7** Place the ravioli on a greased baking sheet and bake for 15 minutes until golden brown. Serve warm, sprinkled with lemon rind, icing (confectioners') sugar and grated chocolate, if you wish.

# PECAN TASSIES

*CREAM CHEESE PASTRY HAS A RICH FLAVOUR THAT GOES WELL WITH THE PECAN FILLING IN THESE TINY TARTLETS, WHICH TAKE THEIR NAME FROM A SCOTTISH WORD MEANING "A SMALL CUP".*

<u>MAKES TWENTY-FOUR</u>

INGREDIENTS
    2 eggs
    175g/6oz/¾ cup firmly packed soft
       dark brown sugar
    5ml/1 tsp vanilla essence (extract)
    large pinch of salt
    25g/1oz/2 tbsp butter, melted
    115g/4oz/1 cup pecan nuts
For the cream cheese pastry
    115g/4oz/½ cup butter
    400g/14oz/1¾ cups cream cheese
    115g/4oz/1 cup plain
       (all-purpose) flour

**1** Place a baking sheet in the oven and preheat to 180°C/350°F/Gas 4. Grease two 12-cup mini muffin or cupcake tins. To make the pastry, cut the butter and cream cheese into pieces and place in a mixing bowl. Sift over the flour and mix to a smooth dough.

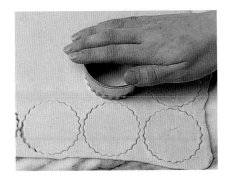

**2** Roll out the dough thinly, then, using a 6cm/2½in fluted pastry cutter, stamp out 24 rounds. Line the mini muffin cups with the rounds and chill.

**3** To make the filling, whisk the eggs in a bowl. Whisk in the brown sugar, a few tablespoons at a time, then add the vanilla, salt and butter. Set aside.

**4** Reserve 24 undamaged pecan halves for the decoration and chop the rest.

**5** Place a spoonful of chopped nuts in each mini muffin cup and cover with the filling. Set a pecan half on the top of each. Bake on the hot baking sheet for about 20 minutes, until puffed and set. Transfer to a rack to cool. Serve at room temperature.

# FILO, ICE CREAM AND MINCEMEAT PARCELS

*LOOKING RATHER LIKE CRISP FRIED PANCAKES, THESE GOLDEN PARCELS REVEAL WARM PIECES OF MINCEMEAT AND MELTING VANILLA ICE CREAM WHEN CUT OPEN. THEY CAN BE ASSEMBLED DAYS IN ADVANCE, READY FOR EASY, LAST-MINUTE FRYING.*

MAKES TWELVE

INGREDIENTS
   1 firm pear, peeled and cored
   225g/8oz/1 cup mincemeat
   finely grated rind of 1 lemon
   12 sheets of filo pastry, thawed
     if frozen
   1 egg, beaten
   250ml/8fl oz/1 cup vanilla ice cream
   oil, for deep-frying
   caster (superfine) sugar, for dusting

**1** Chop the pear and place in a bowl. Stir in the mincemeat and lemon rind.

**2** Keeping the rest of the filo covered under a damp dishtowel, lay one sheet on a board and cut it into two 20cm/8in squares. Brush with beaten egg, then cover with the second square of filo.

**3** Lay 20ml/4 tsp of the mincemeat mixture on the filo, placing it 2.5cm/1in away from one edge and spreading it slightly to cover a 7.5cm/3in area.

**4** Spoon 20ml/4 tsp of the vanilla ice cream over the mincemeat. Brush around the edges of the filo pastry with a little of the remaining beaten egg.

**5** Fold over the two opposite sides of the pastry to cover the filling. Roll up, starting from the filled end. Transfer to a baking sheet and freeze. Make and freeze 11 more rolls in the same way.

**6** Shortly before you are ready to serve, pour oil into a heavy pan to a depth of 7.5cm/3in. Heat it to 185°C/365°F, or until a cube of bread added to the oil browns in 30 seconds.

**7** Fry several parcels at a time for 1–2 minutes until golden, turning them during cooking. Drain on kitchen paper while frying the remainder. Dust with caster sugar and serve immediately.

**VARIATION**
Use mango ice cream instead of vanilla for a sensational change.

# WALNUT AND VANILLA ICE PALMIERS

*THESE WALNUT PASTRIES CAN BE SERVED FRESHLY BAKED, BUT FOR CONVENIENCE, MAKE THEM AHEAD AND REHEAT THEM IN A MEDIUM OVEN FOR 5 MINUTES.*

MAKES SIX

INGREDIENTS
   75g/3oz/¾ cup walnut pieces
   350g/12oz puff pastry
   1 egg, beaten
   45ml/3 tbsp caster (superfine) sugar
   about 200ml/7fl oz/scant 1 cup
     vanilla ice cream

**1** Preheat the oven to 200°C/400°F/ Gas 6. Lightly grease a large baking sheet with butter. Chop the walnuts finely. On a lightly floured surface roll the pastry to a thin rectangle measuring 30 × 20cm/12 × 8in.

**2** Trim the edges of the pastry, then brush with the beaten egg. Sprinkle all but 45ml/3 tbsp of the walnuts and 30ml/2 tbsp of the sugar over the pastry.

**3** Run the rolling pin over the walnuts to press them gently into the pastry, then roll up the pastry from one short edge to the centre, then roll up the other side until the two rolls meet.

**4** Brush the points where the rolls meet with a little beaten egg. Using a sharp knife, cut the pastry into 1cm/½in slices.

**5** Lay the slices on their sides and flatten them with a rolling pin. Transfer to the baking sheet. Brush the slices with more beaten egg and sprinkle with the reserved walnuts and sugar.

**6** Bake for 15 minutes, or until pale golden. Serve the palmiers warm, in pairs, sandwiched with ice cream.

# ALMOND AND DATE FILO PARCELS

*IT IS WORTH BUYING A POT OF GOOD HONEY, SUCH AS ORANGE BLOSSOM OR HEATHER, FOR DIPPING THESE DELICIOUS PASTRIES INTO — IT MAKES ALL THE DIFFERENCE.*

MAKES ABOUT THIRTY

INGREDIENTS
    15ml/1 tbsp sunflower oil
    225g/8oz/2 cups blanched almonds
    115g/4oz/⅔ cup pitted dates
    25g/1oz/2 tbsp butter, softened
    5ml/1 tsp ground cinnamon
    1.5ml/¼ tsp almond essence (extract)
    40g/1½oz/⅓ cup icing
      (confectioners') sugar
    30ml/2 tbsp orange flower water
    10 sheets of filo pastry, thawed
      if frozen
    50g/2oz/¼ cup butter, melted
    120ml/4fl oz/½ cup clear honey
    dates, to serve (optional)

1  Heat the oil in a small pan, add the almonds and fry until golden, stirring constantly. Drain them on kitchen paper, allow to cool, then grind in a very clean coffee or spice mill. Pound the dates by hand or process in a blender or a food processor.

2  Combine the almonds, pitted dates softened butter, cinnamon, almond essence and icing sugar in a mixing bowl, blender or food processor. Add a little orange flower water to taste. Mix or process the mixture to a smooth paste. If the paste feels stiff, work in a little extra flower water, but only 5ml/1 tsp at a time, until smooth.

3  Preheat the oven to 180°C/350°F/ Gas 4. Brush a sheet of filo pastry with melted butter and cut into three equal strips, keeping the remaining sheets covered with a damp dishtowel.

4  Place a walnut-size piece of the almond and date paste at the end of each strip. Fold one corner of the pastry over the filling to make a triangle and then continue folding to make a neat triangular package. Brush with butter. Repeat to make about 30 pastries.

5  Place the pastries on a buttered baking sheet and bake for 30 minutes until golden. Cook them in batches, if possible, as once cooked they must be dipped immediately in honey.

6  While the filo parcels are cooking, pour the clear honey and a little orange flower water into a pan and heat very gently. As soon as the pastries are cooked, lower them one by one into the honey mixture and turn them so that they are coated. Transfer to a plate and cool, then serve, with dates if you like.

# GAZELLES' HORNS

*THESE HORN-SHAPED PASTRIES, FILLED WITH ALMOND PASTE, ARE COMMONLY SERVED AT WEDDING CEREMONIES IN THEIR NATIVE MOROCCO, WHERE THEY ARE A FIRM FAVOURITE.*

MAKES ABOUT SIXTEEN

INGREDIENTS
   200g/7oz/scant 2 cups ground
     almonds
   115g/4oz/1 cup icing
     (confectioners') sugar, plus
     extra for dusting
   30ml/2 tbsp orange flower water
   25g/1oz/2 tbsp butter, melted
   2 egg yolks, beaten
   2.5ml/½ tsp ground cinnamon
For the rich shortcrust pastry
   200g/7oz/1¾ cups plain
     (all-purpose) flour
   pinch of salt
   25g/1oz/2 tbsp butter, melted
   about 30ml/2 tbsp orange
     flower water
   1 egg yolk, beaten
   60–90ml/4–6 tbsp chilled water

**1** Mix the ground almonds, icing sugar, orange flower water, melted butter, egg yolks and cinnamon in a mixing bowl to make a smooth paste.

**2** To make the pastry, sift the flour and salt into a large bowl, then stir in the melted butter, orange flower water and about three-quarters of the egg yolk. Stir in enough chilled water to make a fairly soft dough.

**3** Quickly and lightly, knead the pastry until it is smooth and elastic, then place it on a lightly floured surface and roll it out as thinly as possible. With a sharp knife, cut the dough into long strips about 7.5cm/3in wide.

**4** Preheat the oven to 180°C/350°F/ Gas 4. Roll small pieces of the almond paste into thin sausages about 7.5cm/ 3in long with tapering ends.

**5** Place these in a line along one side of the strips of pastry, about 3cm/1¼in apart. Dampen the pastry edges with water, then fold the other half of the strip over the filling and press the edges together firmly.

**6** Using a pastry wheel, cut around each pastry sausage to make a crescent shape. Make sure that the edges are firmly pinched together.

**7** Prick the crescents with a fork and place on a buttered baking sheet. Brush with the remaining beaten egg yolk and bake for 12–16 minutes until lightly coloured. Allow to cool, then dust with icing sugar.

# BAKLAVA

*THE ORIGINS OF THIS RECIPE LIE IN TURKEY AND GREECE, WHERE THE COFFEE IS BLACK, THICK AND VERY STRONG. COFFEE IS USED IN THIS WELL-KNOWN PASTRY CONFECTION, WHICH IS TRADITIONALLY SERVED ON RELIGIOUS FESTIVAL DAYS, BUT MAKES A LUXURIOUSLY SWEET DESSERT OR TREAT AT ANY TIME. YOU MIGHT LIKE TO OFFER SOME STRONG TURKISH COFFEE WHEN SERVING THIS DESSERT.*

MAKES SIXTEEN

INGREDIENTS
 50g/2oz/½ cup blanched
  almonds, chopped
 50g/2oz/½ cup pistachio
  nuts, chopped
 75g/3oz/6 tbsp caster
  (superfine) sugar
 75g/3oz/6 tbsp butter, melted
 6 sheets of filo pastry, thawed
  if frozen
For the syrup
 115g/4oz/½ cup caster
  (superfine) sugar
 7.5cm/3in piece cinnamon stick
 1 whole clove
 2 green cardamom pods, crushed
 75ml/5 tbsp very strong
  brewed coffee

**1** Preheat the oven to 180°C/350°F/ Gas 4. Add the chopped almonds, nuts and sugar to a small bowl and mix well, stirring to thoroughly coat the nuts in sugar. Brush a shallow 18 × 28cm/ 7 × 11in baking tin with a little of the melted butter.

**2** Using the tin as a guide, cut the six sheets of filo pastry with a very sharp knife so that they fit the tin exactly. It is easiest to cut through all the sheets in one go, rather than working through them singly. Lay a sheet of pastry in the tin and brush it all over with some of the melted butter.

**3** Lay a second sheet of filo in the tin and brush with butter. Add a third sheet, brushing with a little butter. Sprinkle the filo with half of the nut mixture, making sure it is evenly distributed.

**4** Layer three more sheets of filo pastry on top of the nut mixture, brushing each layer with butter as you go. Then spread the remaining nut mixture over the pastry, smoothing it evenly over the entire surface. Top with the remaining sheets of pastry, brushing each sheet with a little more butter as before, and liberally brushing the top layer too. Gently press down with your hand all around the edges to seal.

**COOK'S TIP**
While assembling the baklava, keep the pile of filo pastry sheets covered with a clean damp dishtowel to prevent them from drying out and becoming brittle, which makes the pastry difficult to handle. Work quickly to minimize the risk of the pastry drying out.

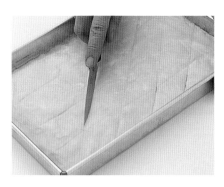

**5** Using a very sharp knife, mark the top of the baklava into diamonds. Place in the preheated oven and bake for 20–25 minutes, or until golden brown and crisp all over.

**6** Meanwhile, make the syrup. Put the sugar, spices and coffee in a small pan and heat gently until the sugar has dissolved – be careful not to burn the sugar as there is a high proportion of it to the liquid. Cover the pan and set aside for 20 minutes, to give the spices time to flavour the syrup.

**7** Remove the baklava from the oven. Reheat the syrup over a gentle heat, then strain it over the pastry, ensuring an even coverage. Leave to cool in the tin. If you can, set it aside for 6 hours or preferably overnight to allow the flavours to mingle. When ready to serve, cut the baklava into diamonds, following the lines scored prior to baking, then remove from the tin.

**VARIATIONS**
• Try different nuts in the baklava filling if you prefer. Walnuts, pecan nuts and hazelnuts can all used to great effect.
• If you would prefer a syrup that does not include coffee, substitute the coffee for 75ml/5 tbsp water and add two strips of thinly pared lemon rind. This will give the baklava a delightful mildly spiced citrus flavour.
• Decorate each baklava diamond with extra nuts if you like.

# WHISKY-LACED MINCE PIES

*MINCEMEAT GETS THE LUXURY TREATMENT WITH THE ADDITION OF GLACÉ PINEAPPLE, CHERRIES AND WHISKY TO MAKE A MARVELLOUS FILLING FOR THESE TRADITIONAL FESTIVE PIES. SERVING THEM WITH A DOLLOP OF WHISKY BUTTER IS PURE INDULGENCE.*

MAKES TWELVE TO FIFTEEN

INGREDIENTS
  225g/8oz/1 cup mincemeat
  50g/2oz/¼ cup glacé (candied)
    pineapple, chopped
  50g/2oz/¼ cup glacé (candied)
    cherries, chopped
  30ml/2 tbsp whisky
  1 egg, beaten or a little milk
  icing (confectioners') sugar,
    for dusting
For the rich shortcrust pastry
  1 egg yolk
  5ml/1 tsp grated orange rind
  15ml/1 tbsp caster
    (superfine) sugar
  225g/8oz/2 cups plain
    (all-purpose) flour
  150g/5oz/⅔ cup butter, diced
For the whisky butter
  75g/3oz/6 tbsp butter, softened
  175g/6oz/1½ cups icing
    (confectioners') sugar, sifted
  30ml/2 tbsp whisky
  5ml/1 tsp grated orange rind

**1** To make the pastry, mix the egg yolk with the orange rind, caster sugar and 10ml/2 tsp chilled water in a small bowl and set aside. Sift the flour into a separate mixing bowl.

**VARIATIONS**
• Use either puff or filo pastry instead of shortcrust for a change.
• Replace the whisky in both the filling and the flavoured butter with Cointreau or brandy, if you like.

**2** Rub or cut in the butter into the flour until the mixture resembles fine breadcrumbs. Stir in the egg mixture and mix to a dough. Wrap in clear film (plastic wrap) and chill for 30 minutes.

**3** Mix the mincemeat, glacé pineapple and cherries in a small bowl. Spoon the whisky over and leave to soak.

**4** Roll out three-quarters of the pastry. Stamp out fluted rounds and use to line 12–15 patty or cupcake tins. Roll out the remaining pastry thinly and stamp out star shapes.

**5** Preheat the oven to 200°C/400°F/ Gas 6. Spoon a little filling into each pastry case and top with a star shape. Brush with a little beaten egg or milk and bake for 20–25 minutes until golden. Leave to cool.

**6** Meanwhile, make the whisky butter. Place the butter, icing sugar, whisky and grated orange rind in a small bowl and beat with a wooden spoon until light and fluffy.

**7** To serve, lift off each pastry star, pipe a whirl of whisky butter on top of the filling, then replace the star. Dust the mince pies with a little icing sugar.

# PEACH AND REDCURRANT TARTLETS

*TART REDCURRANTS AND SWEET PEACHES MAKE A WINNING COMBINATION IN THESE SIMPLE TARTLETS. SMALL BUNCHES OF REDCURRANTS MAKE EASY ORNAMENTS, DUSTED WITH A LITTLE ICING SUGAR.*

MAKES FOUR

INGREDIENTS

25g/1oz/2 tbsp butter, melted
16 sheets of filo pastry, each
    measuring 15cm/6in square, thawed
    if frozen
150ml/¼ pint/⅔ cup double
    (heavy) cream
130g/4½oz peach and mango
    fromage frais or yogurt
vanilla essence (extract)
15ml/1 tbsp icing (confectioners')
    sugar, sifted, plus extra for dusting
2 peaches, halved and stoned (pitted)
50g/2oz/½ cup redcurrants, plus
    redcurrant sprigs, to decorate

**COOK'S TIP**
To strip redcurrants from their stalks,
pull the stalks through the tines of a fork
so that they drop into a bowl.

1  Preheat the oven to 190°C/375°F/ Gas 5. Use a little of the butter to lightly grease four individual tartlet tins (mini quiche pans). Brush the pastry squares with a little more butter, stack them in fours, then place in the tartlet tins to make four pastry cases. Bake for about 15 minutes until golden. Cool the filo cases on a wire rack before removing them from the tins.

2  To make the filling, whip the cream to soft peaks, then lightly fold in the fromage frais or yogurt with a few drops of the vanilla essence and icing sugar. Divide among the pastry cases.

3  Slice the peaches and arrange the slices on top of the filling, with a few redcurrants. Decorate with redcurrant sprigs and dust with icing sugar.

# TIA MARIA TRUFFLE TARTLETS

*SOPHISTICATED AND SERIOUSLY INDULGENT, THESE MINI COFFEE PASTRY CASES ARE FILLED WITH A CHOCOLATE LIQUEUR TRUFFLE CENTRE AND TOPPED WITH FRESH RIPE BERRIES.*

## SERVES SIX

### INGREDIENTS
300ml/½ pint/1¼ cups double
  (heavy) cream
225g/8oz/generous ¾ cup seedless
  blackberry or raspberry jam
150g/5oz plain (semisweet)
  chocolate, broken up
45ml/3 tbsp Tia Maria liqueur
450g/1lb/4 cups mixed berries
For the coffee-flavoured pastry
  225g/8oz/2 cups plain
    (all-purpose) flour
  15ml/1 tbsp caster (superfine) sugar
  150g/5oz/⅔ cup butter, diced
  1 egg yolk
  30ml/2 tbsp very strong brewed
    coffee, chilled

**1** Preheat the oven to 200°C/400°F/ Gas 6, placing a large baking sheet in the oven to heat. To make the pastry, sift the flour and sugar into a large bowl. Rub or cut in the butter until the mixture resembles fine breadcrumbs. Blend the egg yolk with the coffee, add to the bowl and mix to a stiff dough. Knead on a floured surface for a few seconds until smooth. Wrap in clear film (plastic wrap) and chill for 20 minutes.

**2** Roll out the pastry and use to line six 10cm/4in fluted tartlet tins (mini quiche pans). Prick the bases with a fork and line with foil and baking beans. Place on the hot baking sheet and bake for 10 minutes. Remove the foil and beans, and bake for a further 8–10 minutes. Allow to cool in the tins.

**3** To make the filling, slowly bring the cream and 175g/6oz/generous ½ cup of the jam to the boil, stirring constantly.

**4** Remove the pan from the heat, add the chocolate and 30ml/2 tbsp of the liqueur. Stir until melted. Leave to cool, then spoon the mixture into the pastry cases, and smooth the tops. Place on a baking tray and chill for 40 minutes.

**5** Heat the remaining jam and liqueur and stir until smooth. Arrange the fruit on the tarts, then brush the jam glaze over. Chill until ready to serve.

**COOK'S TIP**
When making the pastry, the yolk and coffee must be blended together until very well mixed to ensure that the pastry is evenly coloured.

# POACHED PEAR TARTLETS
## WITH CHOCOLATE SAUCE

*PUFF PASTRY IS SHAPED AND TOPPED WITH SPICY POACHED PEARS. THE CHOCOLATE SAUCE COMPLEMENTS THE PASTRIES BEAUTIFULLY.*

SERVES SIX

INGREDIENTS
    3 firm pears, peeled
    450ml/¾ pint/scant 2 cups water
    strip of thinly pared orange rind
    1 vanilla pod (bean)
    1 bay leaf
    50g/2oz/¼ cup granulated sugar
    350g/12oz puff pastry
    40g/1½oz/⅓ cup cocoa
      powder (unsweetened)
    75ml/5 tbsp double (heavy) cream
    15g/½oz/1 tbsp butter, softened
    15ml/1 tbsp soft light brown sugar
    25g/1oz/¼ cup walnuts, chopped
    1 egg, beaten
    15g/½oz/1 tbsp caster (superfine) sugar

**1** Cut the pears in half and scoop out just the cores with a melon baller or small spoon.

**2** Put the water in a small pan with the orange rind, vanilla pod, bay leaf and sugar. Bring to the boil, stirring well. Add the pears and more water to cover.

**3** Cover and cook very gently for about 15 minutes, or until just tender. Remove the pears with a slotted spoon and set aside to cool slightly while you make the pastry. Reserve the syrup.

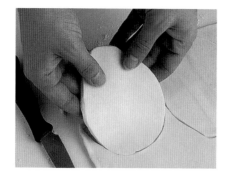

**4** Meanwhile, roll out the pastry on a lightly floured work surface and cut out six pear shapes, slightly larger than the pear halves. Place the pastry shapes on greased baking sheets and chill for 30 minutes.

**5** Remove the orange rind, vanilla pod and bay leaf from the reserved syrup, then return the syrup to the heat and boil rapidly for 10 minutes. Blend the cocoa powder with 60ml/4 tbsp cold water in a separate pan.

**6** Stir a few spoonfuls of the syrup into the cocoa paste, then whisk the paste into the syrup in the pan. Continue to cook until reduced to about 150ml/ ¼ pint/⅔ cup. Remove the pan from the heat and add the cream to the syrup. Stir well.

**7** Preheat the oven to 200°C/400°F/ Gas 6. In a bowl, mix together the butter, sugar and walnuts. Gently pat the pears dry with kitchen paper, then spoon a little filling into each cavity.

**8** Lightly brush the pastry pear shapes with a little beaten egg. Put a pear half, filled side down, in the centre of each pastry shape.

**9** Lightly sprinkle the pastries with a little caster sugar. Bake for 12 minutes, or until the pastry has puffed up around the pear and is golden brown. Drizzle over some of the warm chocolate sauce and serve immediately.

**COOK'S TIP**
Decorate these tartlets with small fresh bay leaves, if you wish.

# APRICOT FILO PURSES

*THESE LITTLE FILO PARCELS CONCEAL A DELECTABLE APRICOT AND MINCEMEAT FILLING. THEY PROVIDE THE PERFECT EXCUSE FOR USING UP ANY MINCEMEAT AND MARZIPAN.*

MAKES EIGHT

INGREDIENTS
   350g/12oz filo pastry, thawed
      if frozen
   50g/2oz/¼ cup butter, melted
   8 apricots, halved and
      stoned (pitted)
   60ml/4 tbsp mincemeat
   12 ratafia biscuits (almond
      macaroons), crushed
   30ml/2 tbsp grated marzipan
   icing (confectioners') sugar,
      for dusting

**COOK'S TIP**
Filo pastry dries out quickly, so keep any squares not currently being used covered under a clean damp dishtowel.

**1** Preheat the oven to 200°C/400°F/ Gas 6. Cut the sheets of filo pastry into 32 squares, each about 18cm/7in. Brush four of the squares with a little melted butter and stack them, giving each layer a quarter turn to create a star shape. Repeat with the remaining filo squares to make eight stars.

**2** Place an apricot half, hollow side up, in the centre of each pastry star. Mix the mincemeat, crushed ratafias and marzipan together and spoon a little of the mixture into the hollow in each apricot half.

**3** Top with another apricot half, then bring the corners of each pastry star together and gently squeeze to make a gathered purse.

**4** Place the purses on a baking sheet and brush each with a little melted butter. Bake for about 20 minutes, or until the pastry is golden and crisp. Lightly dust with icing sugar and serve the purses immediately. Whipped cream, flavoured with a little brandy, makes an ideal accompaniment.

# COFFEE CREAM PROFITEROLES

*CRISP-TEXTURED COFFEE CHOUX PASTRY PUFFS ARE FILLED WITH CREAM AND DRIZZLED WITH A WHITE CHOCOLATE SAUCE. FOR THOSE WITH A SWEET TOOTH, THERE IS PLENTY OF EXTRA SAUCE.*

SERVES SIX

INGREDIENTS

50g/2oz/¼ cup granulated sugar
100ml/3¾fl oz/scant ½ cup water
150g/5oz good quality white
   chocolate, broken up
25g/1oz/2 tbsp butter
300ml/½ pint/1¼ cups double
   (heavy) cream
30ml/2 tbsp coffee liqueur, such as
   Tia Maria or Kahlúa
For the coffee choux pastry
65g/2½oz/9 tbsp plain
   (all-purpose) flour
pinch of salt
50g/2oz/¼ cup butter, diced
150ml/¼ pint/⅔ cup freshly
   brewed coffee
2 eggs, lightly beaten

**1** Preheat the oven to 220°C/425°F/ Gas 7. To make the pastry, sift the flour and salt on to a sheet of baking parchment and set aside. Put the butter into a pan with the coffee. Bring to a rolling boil, then remove the pan from the heat and tip in all the flour. Beat vigorously with a wooden spoon until the mixture forms a ball and comes away from the sides of the pan. Leave to cool for 2 minutes.

**2** Gradually add the beaten eggs to the flour mixture, beating thoroughly after each addition, until they are fully incorporated and you have a smooth consistency. Spoon the mixture into a piping (pastry) bag fitted with a 1cm/ ½in plain nozzle.

**3** Pipe about 24 small buns on to a dampened baking sheet. Bake for about 20 minutes, then transfer to a wire rack. Pierce each bun with a knife to let out the steam. Leave the buns to cool.

**4** To make the sauce, put the sugar and water in a pan and heat gently until the sugar has dissolved. Bring to the boil, then simmer for about 3 minutes. Remove the pan from the heat and add the chocolate and butter, stirring until smooth. Stir in 45ml/3 tbsp of the cream and the coffee liqueur. Keep warm or cool to room temperature.

**5** To assemble, whip the remaining cream in a small bowl until soft peaks form. Spoon the cream into a piping bag and use to fill the buns through the slits in the sides. Pile on a large plate and pour a little sauce over. Serve the remaining sauce separately.

# SWEET TARTS AND PIES

Some sweet pies are so popular that they are eaten and enjoyed all over the world. Classics like Deep-dish Apple Pie and Mississippi Mud Pie come into this category, along with Key Lime Pie and Linzertorte. Newer ideas with a modern twist include Fresh Orange Tart. Some dishes, such as Peach Leaf Pie, are topped with pastry shapes that hint at what lies beneath, others have lattice tops, a few conceal their fillings under swirls of meringue, but all are delectable.

# DATE AND ALMOND TART

*FRESH DATES MAKE AN UNUSUAL BUT DELICIOUS FILLING FOR A TART, ESPECIALLY WHEN TEAMED WITH A SPONGE FILLING FLAVOURED WITH GROUND ALMONDS AND ORANGE FLOWER WATER.*

**SERVES SIX**

INGREDIENTS
  90g/3½oz/scant ½ cup butter
  90g/3½oz/scant ½ cup caster
    (superfine) sugar
  1 egg, beaten
  90g/3½oz/scant 1 cup
    ground almonds
  30ml/2 tbsp plain (all-purpose) flour
  30ml/2 tbsp orange flower water
  12–13 fresh dates, halved and
    stoned (pitted)
  60ml/4 tbsp apricot jam
For the rich shortcrust pastry
  175g/6oz/1½ cups plain
    (all-purpose) flour
  75g/3oz/6 tbsp butter, diced
  1 egg
  15ml/1 tbsp chilled water

**2** Roll out the pastry on a lightly floured surface and use to line a 20cm/8in flan tin (quiche pan). Prick the base with a fork, then chill until required.

**3** Cream the butter and sugar in a small mixing bowl with a wooden spoon until light, then beat in the egg. Stir in the ground almonds, flour and 15ml/ 1 tbsp of the orange flower water and mix thoroughly.

**4** Spread the almond filling evenly over the base of the pastry case. Arrange the dates, cut side down, on the mixture. Bake the tart on the hot baking sheet for 10–15 minutes, then lower the oven temperature to 180°C/350°F/Gas 4. Bake for 15 minutes more, or until pale golden and set.

**1** Preheat the oven to 200°C/400°F/ Gas 6 and place a baking sheet in it to preheat. To make the pastry, sift the flour into a bowl, then rub or cut in the butter until the mixture resembles fine breadcrumbs. Add the egg and water, then work to a dough. Wrap in clear film (plastic wrap) and chill for 20 minutes.

**5** Transfer the tart to a wire rack to cool. Meanwhile, in a small pan, gently heat the apricot jam, then press through a sieve into a bowl. Stir in the remaining orange flower water. Lightly brush the apricot glaze over the tart and serve at room temperature.

# BLUEBERRY FRANGIPANE FLAN

*THERE'S SOMETHING IRRESISTIBLE ABOUT THIS TANGY LEMON PASTRY CASE WITH ITS SWEET ALMOND FILLING AND RINGS OF RIPE BLUEBERRIES. THE JAM AND LIQUEUR GLAZE ADDS AN INDULGENT FINISH.*

SERVES SIX

INGREDIENTS

    30ml/2 tbsp ground coffee
    45ml/3 tbsp near-boiling milk
    50g/2oz/¼ cup butter
    50g/2oz/¼ cup caster
      (superfine) sugar
    1 egg
    115g/4oz/1 cup ground almonds
    15ml/1 tbsp plain (all-purpose) flour
    225g/8oz/2 cups blueberries
    30ml/2 tbsp seedless blackberry jam
    15ml/1 tbsp Amaretto liqueur
    crème fraîche or sour cream, to serve
For the shortcrust pastry
    175g/6oz/1½ cups plain
      (all-purpose) flour
    115g/4oz/½ cup butter, diced
    25g/1oz/2 tbsp caster
      (superfine) sugar
    finely grated rind of ½ lemon
    15ml/1 tbsp chilled water

**1** Preheat the oven to 190°F/375°C/ Gas 5. To make the pastry, sift the flour into a large bowl and rub or cut in the butter until the mixture resembles fine breadcrumbs. Add the caster sugar and lemon rind, stir well, then add the water and mix to a firm dough. Wrap the pastry in clear film (plastic wrap) and chill for 20 minutes.

**2** Roll out the pastry on a lightly floured surface and use to line a 23cm/9in loose-based flan tin (quiche pan). Prick the base with a fork. Line the pastry with baking parchment and baking beans and bake for 10 minutes.

**3** Remove the baking parchment and beans and bake for 10 minutes more. Remove the pastry case from the oven.

**4** Meanwhile, mix the coffee and milk in a large mixing bowl. Leave to infuse for 4 minutes. Cream the butter and sugar until pale. Beat in the egg, then add the almonds and flour. Strain in the milky coffee through a fine sieve and gently fold it in.

**5** Spoon the coffee mixture into the pastry case and spread evenly. Scatter the blueberries over the top and push them down slightly into the mixture. Bake for about 30 minutes until firm, covering with foil after 20 minutes.

**6** Remove from the oven and allow to cool slightly. Melt the jam and liqueur in a small pan and brush over the flan. Remove from the tin and serve warm.

# RASPBERRY AND CRÈME BRÛLÉE TART

*FRESH RASPBERRIES AND A CRUNCHY CARAMEL TOPPING CONTRAST WITH THE THICK VANILLA-SCENTED CUSTARD FILLING IN THIS LOVELY SUMMERY TART.*

SERVES EIGHT

INGREDIENTS
  1 vanilla pod (bean)
  450ml/¾ pint/scant 2 cups double
    (heavy) cream
  1 whole egg, plus 3 egg yolks
  30ml/2 tbsp caster (superfine) sugar
  150g/5oz/scant 1 cup
    fresh raspberries
  5 tbsp icing (confectioners') sugar
For the pâte sucrée
  150g/5oz/1¼ cups plain
    (all-purpose) flour
  pinch of salt
  25g/1oz/¼ cup icing
    (confectioners') sugar
  75g/3oz/6 tbsp butter, diced
  2 egg yolks
  finely grated rind of 1 orange
  15ml/1 tbsp egg white, lightly beaten

**1** To make the pastry, sift the flour, salt and icing sugar into a mixing bowl. Rub or cut in the butter until the mixture resembles fine breadcrumbs.

**2** Mix the egg yolks and orange rind together, add to the dry ingredients and mix to a soft dough. Knead on a lightly floured work surface for a few seconds, until smooth. Wrap in clear film (plastic wrap) and chill for 30 minutes.

**3** Roll out the pastry and use to line a fluted 23cm/9in flan tin (quiche pan). Cover and chill for a further 30 minutes. While the pastry case is chilling, put a baking sheet in the oven and preheat to 200°C/400°F/Gas 6.

**4** Prick the base of the pastry all over with a fork and line with foil and baking beans. Place on the hot baking sheet and bake blind for 10 minutes. Remove the foil and beans and bake the pastry for 5 minutes more.

**5** Lightly brush the base and sides of the pastry case with egg white, then return to the oven for 3–4 minutes. Lower the oven temperature to 160°C/325°F/Gas 3.

**6** Halve the vanilla pod lengthways. Place in a small pan with the cream. Slowly bring to the boil, then remove the vanilla pod. In a mixing bowl or pouring jug (pitcher), whisk the egg and egg yolks with the sugar until pale. Slowly whisk in the hot cream.

**7** Sprinkle the raspberries over the base of the pastry case, arranging them so that they are fairly evenly distributed. Pour over the custard, then bake the tart for 17–20 minutes, or until very lightly set. Place on a wire rack to cool. Chill for at least 4 hours, or overnight.

**8** To add the crunchy caramel topping, first protect the edges of the pastry case with pieces of foil. Dredge a thin layer of icing sugar over the custard, right to the edge of the pastry case. Place under a hot grill (broiler) for 1 minute, or until the sugar melts and turns a dark golden colour. Take care not to over-grill or the custard will separate. Chill for about 10 minutes, to allow the caramel to harden slightly, then serve in slices.

# ALSACE PLUM TART

*FRUIT AND CUSTARD TARTS ARE TYPICAL OF THE ALSACE REGION OF FRANCE. SOME HAVE A YEAST DOUGH BASE INSTEAD OF PASTRY. USE OTHER SEASONAL FRUITS OR A MIXTURE IF YOU LIKE.*

SERVES SIX TO EIGHT

INGREDIENTS
    450g/1lb ripe plums, halved
      and stoned (pitted)
    30ml/2 tbsp Kirsch or plum brandy
    30ml/2 tbsp seedless raspberry jam
    2 eggs
    50g/2oz/¼ cup caster
      (superfine) sugar
    175ml/6fl oz/¾ cup double
      (heavy) cream
    grated rind of ½ lemon
    1.5ml/¼ tsp vanilla essence (extract)
For the pâte sucrée
    200g/7oz/1¾ cups plain
      (all-purpose) flour
    pinch of salt
    25g/1oz/¼ cup icing
      (confectioners') sugar
    100g/3½oz/scant ½ cup butter, diced
    2 egg yolks
    15ml/1 tbsp chilled water

**1** To make the pastry, sift the flour, salt and sugar into a bowl. Rub or cut in the butter until the mixture resembles fine breadcrumbs. Mix the egg yolks and water together, sprinkle over the dry ingredients and mix to a soft dough.

**2** Lightly knead on a floured work surface for a few seconds until smooth. Wrap in clear film (plastic wrap) and chill for 30 minutes.

**4** Roll out the pastry thinly and use to line a 23cm/9in flan tin (quiche pan). Cover and chill for 30 minutes. Prick the base all over with a fork and line with foil. Add a layer of baking beans and bake for 15 minutes until slightly dry and set. Remove the foil and beans.

**6** Lower the oven temperature to 180°C/350°F/Gas 4. Beat the eggs and sugar until well combined, then beat in the cream, lemon rind, vanilla essence and any juice from the plums.

**3** Preheat the oven to 200°C/400°F/ Gas 6. Mix the plums with the Kirsch or plum brandy in a bowl and set aside for 30 minutes.

**5** Lightly brush the base of the pastry case with a thin layer of jam, bake for 5 minutes more, then transfer to a wire rack to cool.

**7** Arrange the plums, cut side down, in the pastry case, then pour over the custard mixture. Bake for 30 minutes, or until a knife inserted in the centre comes out clean. Serve the tart warm.

# CARAMELIZED UPSIDE-DOWN PEAR PIE

*IN THIS GLORIOUSLY STICKY DESSERT, THE PASTRY IS BAKED ON TOP OF THE FRUIT, WHICH GIVES IT A CRISP AND FLAKY TEXTURE. WHEN INVERTED, THE PIE LOOKS WONDERFUL.*

SERVES EIGHT

INGREDIENTS
5–6 firm, ripe pears
175g/6oz/¾ cup caster
(superfine) sugar
115g/4oz/½ cup butter
whipped cream, to serve
For the shorcrust pastry
115g/4oz/1 cup plain
(all-purpose) flour
1.5ml/¼ tsp salt
130g/4½oz/9 tbsp cold butter, diced
40g/1½oz/3 tbsp white vegetable
fat, diced
60ml/4 tbsp chilled water

**1** To make the pastry, combine the flour and salt in a bowl. Cut or rub in the butter and vegetable fat until the mixture resembles coarse breadcrumbs. Stir in just enough water to bind. Wrap the dough in clear film (plastic wrap) and chill for 30 minutes. Preheat the oven to 200°C/400°F/Gas 6.

**2** Peel, quarter and core the pears. Toss with some of the sugar in a bowl.

**3** Melt the butter in a 27cm/10½in heavy ovenproof omelette pan. Add the remaining sugar. When it changes colour, arrange the pears in the pan.

**4** Continue cooking, uncovered, for about 20 minutes, or until the fruit has completely caramelized.

**5** Leave the fruit to cool in the pan. Meanwhile, on a lightly floured surface, roll out the pastry to a round that is slightly larger than the diameter of the pan. Place the pastry on top of the pears and carefully tuck the pastry in around the edges.

**6** Bake for 15 minutes, then lower the oven temperature to 180°C/350°F/Gas 4. Bake for a further 15 minutes, or until the pastry is golden.

**7** Let the pie cool in the pan for a few minutes. To unmould, run a knife around the pan's edge, then, using oven gloves, invert a plate over the pan and quickly turn the two over together.

**8** If any pears stick to the pan, remove them gently with a metal spatula and replace them carefully on the pie. Serve warm in slices with a little whipped cream, if you like.

VARIATIONS
• To make Caramelized Upside-down Apple Pie, replace the pears with 8–9 firm, tart apples – Cox's Orange Pippins would be a good choice. You will need more apples than pears as they shrink during cooking.
• Nectarines or peaches also work well, as does rhubarb. Rhubarb is tart, so you may need more sugar.
• For a more exotic pie, use sliced mango.
• Children like banana upside-down pie. Buy small bananas, peel them and slice them in half lengthways, then arrange the slices in the pan.

# EXOTIC FRUIT TRANCHE

*THIS IS A GOOD WAY TO MAKE THE MOST OF A SMALL SELECTION OF EXOTIC FRUIT.*

SERVES EIGHT

INGREDIENTS

150ml/¼ pint/⅓ cup double (heavy)
    cream, plus extra to serve
250g/9oz/generous 1 cup mascarpone
    cheese
25g/1oz/¼ cup icing (confectioners')
    sugar, sifted
grated rind of 1 orange
450g/1lb/3 cups mixed prepared
    seasonal fruits
90ml/6 tbsp apricot conserve, sieved
15ml/1 tbsp white or coconut rum
For the rich shortcrust pastry
175g/6oz/1½ cups plain
    (all-purpose) flour
50g/2oz/¼ cup butter, diced
25g/1oz/2 tbsp white vegetable fat
50g/2oz/¼ cup caster
    (superfine) sugar
2 egg yolks
about 15ml/1 tbsp chilled water
115g/4oz/scant ½ cup apricot
    conserve, sieved and warmed

**1** To make the pastry, sift the flour into a large mixing bowl and rub or cut in the fat until the mixture resembles fine breadcrumbs. Stir in the caster sugar. Add the egg yolks and enough chilled water to make a soft dough.

**2** Roll out the pastry thinly between two sheets of clear film (plastic wrap) and use to line a 35 × 12cm/14 × 4½in fluted tranche tin. Allow the excess pastry to hang over the edge of the tin and chill for 30 minutes.

**3** Preheat the oven to 200°C/400°F/ Gas 6. Prick the base of the pastry case and line with baking parchment and baking beans. Bake for 10–12 minutes. Lift out the paper and beans and return the pastry to the oven for 5 minutes. Trim off the excess pastry and brush the inside of the case with the warmed apricot conserve to form a seal. Leave to cool on a wire rack.

**4** Whip the cream to soft peaks, then stir it into the mascarpone with the icing sugar and orange rind. Spread evenly in the cooled pastry case and top with the prepared fruits. Gently warm the apricot conserve with the rum in a pan, and drizzle or brush over the fruits to make a glaze. Serve with extra cream.

**COOK'S TIPS**
• Use fruits such as mango, papaya, star fruit, kiwi fruit and blackberries
• If you don't have a tranche tin, use a 23cm/9in flan tin (quiche pan).

# FRESH ORANGE TART

*FINELY GRATED ORANGE RIND GIVES THIS RICH SHORTCRUST PASTRY ITS WONDERFUL COLOUR AND FLAVOUR. A CREAMY CUSTARD FILLING AND FRESH ORANGES TURN IT INTO A SOPHISTICATED DESSERT.*

## SERVES NINE

INGREDIENTS
  2 eggs, plus 2 egg yolks
  150g/5oz/⅔ cup caster
    (superfine) sugar
  150ml/¼ pint/⅔ cup single
    (light) cream
  finely grated rind and juice
    of 1 orange
  6–8 oranges
  fresh mint sprigs, to decorate
For the rich shortcrust pastry
  175g/6oz/1½ cups plain
    (all-purpose) flour
  90g/3½oz/scant ½ cup butter, diced
  15ml/1 tbsp caster (superfine) sugar
  finely grated rind of 1 orange
  1 egg yolk
  about 10ml/2 tsp orange juice

**1** To make the pastry, sift the flour and rub or cut in the butter. Stir in the sugar and orange rind. Beat the egg yolk with the orange juice, then add to the dry ingredients and mix to a firm dough.

**2** Lightly and quickly knead the dough until smooth. Roll out and use to line a 20cm/8in square fluted tin. Wrap and chill for 30 minutes.

**3** Put a baking sheet in the oven and preheat to 200°C/400°F/Gas 6. Prick the pastry case all over with a fork and line with foil and baking beans. Place on the hot baking sheet and bake blind for 12 minutes. Remove the foil and beans and bake the pastry for a further 5 minutes.

**4** Whisk the eggs, yolks and sugar in a bowl until foamy. Whisk in the cream, followed by the orange rind and juice. Pour into the pastry case and bake for 30–35 minutes until firm. Remove from the oven and leave to cool on a wire rack still in the tin.

**5** Peel the oranges, removing all the white pith and separate the segments by cutting between the membranes. Arrange the segments in rows on top of the tart. Chill until ready to serve, then carefully remove the tart from the tin and decorate with sprigs of fresh mint.

# PEACH LEAF PIE

*JUICY, LIGHTLY SPICED PEACH SLICES ARE COVERED WITH A CRUST MADE ENTIRELY FROM INDIVIDUAL PASTRY LEAVES TO MAKE THIS SPECTACULAR PIE.*

SERVES EIGHT

INGREDIENTS
    1.2kg/2½lb ripe peaches
    juice of 1 lemon
    115g/4oz/½ cup granulated sugar
    45ml/3 tbsp cornflour (cornstarch)
    1.5ml/¼ tsp grated nutmeg
    2.5ml/½ tsp ground cinnamon
    25g/1oz/2 tbsp butter, diced
    1 egg, beaten with 45ml/1 tbsp
        water, to glaze
For the shortcrust pastry
    225g/8oz/2 cups plain
        (all-purpose) flour
    4ml/¾ tsp salt
    115g/4oz/½ cup cold butter, diced
    40g/1½oz/3 tbsp white vegetable
        fat, diced
    75–90ml/5–6 tbsp chilled water

**1**  To make the pastry, sift the flour and salt into a large mixing bowl. Add the butter and vegetable fat, and rub in with your fingertips or cut in with a pastry blender until the mixture resembles coarse breadcrumbs.

**2**  Sprinkle over the dry ingredients just enough of the water to bind the mixture and use a fork to bring it together to form a soft dough. Gather the dough into two balls, one slightly larger than the other. Wrap separately in clear film (plastic wrap) and chill for 30 minutes. Meanwhile, put a baking sheet in the oven and preheat to 220°C/425°F/Gas 7.

**3**  Drop a few peaches at a time into a large pan of boiling water, leave for 20 seconds, then transfer to a bowl of cold water. When cool, peel. Slice the peaches and mix with the lemon juice, sugar, cornflour and spices. Set aside.

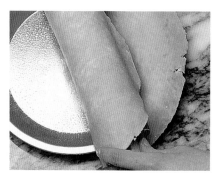

**4**  On a lightly floured surface, roll out the larger piece of pastry to a thickness of 3mm/⅛in. Use to line a 23cm/9in pie plate. Chill until required.

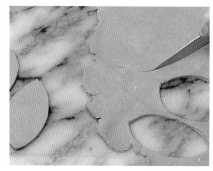

**5**  Roll out the second piece of pastry and cut out leaf shapes about 7.5cm/3in long. Cut out enough to completely cover the top. Mark veins with a knife.

**6**  Brush the base of the pastry case with egg glaze. Add the peach mixture, piling it into a dome in the centre. Dot with the butter.

**7**  To assemble the pie top, start from the outside edge. Make a ring of leaves around the edge attaching each leaf to the pastry base with a dab of egg glaze. Place a second ring of leaves above, staggering the positions. Continue with rows of leaves until the pie is covered. Brush with egg glaze.

**8**  Bake the pie on the hot baking sheet for about 10 minutes. Lower the oven temperature to 180°C/350°F/Gas 4 and continue to bake for 35–40 minutes more, or until golden. Serve hot, with cream, if you like.

**COOK'S TIP**
Baking the pie on a hot baking sheet helps to make the pastry case crisp on the base. The moisture from the filling might otherwise cause the pastry to become soggy.

# DEEP-DISH APPLE PIE

*THIS ALL-TIME CLASSIC FAVOURITE IS MADE WITH RICH SHORTCRUST PASTRY. INSIDE, SUGAR, SPICES AND FLOUR CREATE A DELICIOUSLY THICK AND SYRUPY SAUCE WITH THE APPLE JUICES.*

**4** Put a baking sheet in the oven and preheat to 200°C/400°F/Gas 6. Roll out just over half the pastry and use to line a 23cm/9in pie dish that is 4cm/1½in deep, allowing the pastry to overhang the edges slightly. Spoon in the filling, doming the apple slices in the centre.

**5** Roll out the remaining pastry to form the lid. Lightly brush the edges of the pastry case with a little water, then place the lid over the apple filling.

**6** Trim the pastry with a sharp knife. Gently press the edges together to seal, then knock up the edge. Re-roll the pastry trimmings and cut out apple and leaf shapes. Brush the top of the pie with egg white. Arrange the pastry apples and leaves on top.

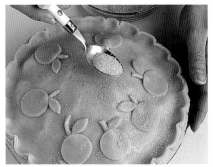

**7** Brush again with egg white, then sprinkle with golden granulated sugar. Make two small slits in the top of the pie to allow steam to escape.

**8** Bake for 30 minutes, then lower the oven temperature to 180°C/350°F/Gas 4 and bake for a further 15 minutes until the pastry is golden and the apples are soft – check by inserting a small sharp knife or skewer through one of the slits in the top of the pie. Serve hot, with some whipped cream.

SERVES SIX

INGREDIENTS
115g/4oz/½ cup caster
  (superfine) sugar
45ml/3 tbsp plain (all-purpose) flour
2.5ml/½ tsp ground cinnamon
finely grated rind of 1 orange
900g/2lb tart cooking apples
1 egg white, lightly beaten
30ml/2 tbsp golden granulated sugar
whipped cream, to serve
For the shortcrust pastry
350g/12oz/3 cups plain
  (all-purpose) flour
pinch of salt
175g/6oz/¾ cup butter, diced
about 75ml/5 tbsp chilled water

**1** To make the pastry, sift the flour and salt into a mixing bowl and rub or cut in the butter until the mixture resembles fine breadcrumbs.

**2** Sprinkle over the water and mix to a firm, soft dough. Knead lightly for a few seconds until smooth. Wrap in clear film (plastic wrap) and chill for 30 minutes.

**3** Combine the caster sugar, flour, cinnamon and orange rind in a bowl. Peel, core and thinly slice the apples. Add to the sugar mixture in the bowl, then toss gently with your fingertips until they are all evenly coated.

# ONE-CRUST RHUBARB PIE

*THIS METHOD CAN BE USED FOR ALL SORTS OF FRUIT AND IS REALLY FOOLPROOF. IT DOESN'T MATTER HOW ROUGH THE PIE LOOKS WHEN IT GOES INTO THE OVEN; IT COMES OUT LOOKING FANTASTIC!*

**4** Cut the rhubarb into pieces about 2.5cm/1in and place in a large bowl. Add the sugar and ginger and mix well.

**5** Pile the rhubarb mixture into the middle of the pastry round. Carefully draw the pastry up roughly around the filling so that it encloses it but does not cover it completely. Some of the fruit should remain visible in the centre.

**6** Lightly glaze the pastry rim with any remaining egg yolk and sprinkle the chopped hazelnuts and golden sugar over. Bake for 30–35 minutes, or until the pastry is golden brown. Serve warm.

## SERVES SIX

INGREDIENTS
  1 egg yolk, beaten
  25g/1oz/3 tbsp semolina
  450g/1lb rhubarb
  75g/3oz/6 tbsp caster
    (superfine) sugar
  1–2 pieces stem (crystallized) ginger
    in syrup, drained and
    finely chopped
  25g/1oz/¼ cup chopped hazelnuts
  30ml/2 tbsp golden granulated sugar
For the shortcrust pastry
  225g/8oz/2 cups plain
    (all-purpose) flour
  pinch of salt
  115g/4oz/½ cup butter, diced
  45–60ml/3–4 tbsp chilled water

**1** To make the pastry, sift the flour and salt into a small bowl. Rub or cut in the butter until the mixture resembles fine breadcrumbs. Sprinkle over 45ml/3 tbsp of the water and mix together to a soft dough, adding more water if needed. Wrap in clear film (plastic wrap) and chill for 30 minutes.

**2** Preheat the oven to 200°C/400°F/ Gas 6. On a lightly floured surface, roll out the pastry to a 35cm/14in round. Lay it over the rolling pin and transfer it to a large baking sheet.

**3** Brush a little egg yolk over the pastry round. Sprinkle the semolina evenly over the centre of the pastry, leaving a wide margin all round.

**COOK' TIP**
Egg yolk glaze brushed on to the pastry gives it a nice golden sheen. However, be careful not to let the glaze drip on to the baking sheet, or it will burn and be difficult to remove.

# LINZERTORTE

*USE A GOOD QUALITY JAM OR CONSERVE TO FILL THE CINNAMON AND ALMOND PASTRY CASE IN THIS TRADITIONAL AUSTRIAN SPECIALITY, AND DUST IT WITH ICING SUGAR BEFORE SERVING.*

SERVES EIGHT TO TEN

INGREDIENTS
200g/7oz/scant 1 cup butter
200g/7oz/scant 1 cup caster
  (superfine) sugar
3 eggs, plus 2 egg yolks
2.5ml/½ tsp ground cinnamon
grated rind of ½ lemon
115g/4oz/2 cups fine sweet biscuit
  (cookie) crumbs
150g/5oz/1¼ cups ground almonds
225g/8oz/2 cups plain (all-purpose)
  flour, sifted
225g/8oz/¾ cup raspberry jam
icing (confectioners') sugar,
  for dusting

**1** Preheat the oven to 190°C/375°F/ Gas 5. Cream the butter and sugar together until light. Slowly add the eggs and 1 of the egg yolks, beating all the time, then add the cinnamon and rind.

**2** Stir the crumbs and ground almonds into the mixture. Mix well, then add the sifted flour. Knead the mixture to form a dough, then wrap in clear film (plastic wrap) and chill for about 30 minutes.

**3** Roll out two-thirds of the pastry on a lightly floured surface and use to line a deep 25cm/10in loose-based flan tin (quiche pan). Press the pastry into the sides and trim the edge.

**4** Spread the raspberry jam generously and evenly over the base of the pastry case. Roll out the remaining pastry into a long rectangle. Cut this into even strips with a sharp knife and arrange in a lattice pattern over the jam filling.

**5** Lightly beat the remaining egg yolk in a small bowl, then brush it evenly over the pastry rim and lattice. Bake the flan for 45 minutes, or until golden brown. Leave to cool in the tin before turning out on to a wire rack. Just before serving, sift a little icing sugar over the top of the Linzertorte. Serve with custard, if you like.

# ITALIAN CHOCOLATE RICOTTA TART

*CREAMY RICOTTA CHEESE PACKED WITH MIXED PEEL AND DARK CHOCOLATE CHIPS IS BAKED IN A CHOCOLATE AND SHERRY PASTRY CASE FOR MAXIMUM FLAVOUR.*

SERVES SIX

INGREDIENTS

2 egg yolks
115g/4oz/½ cup caster
  (superfine) sugar
500g/1¼lb/2½ cups ricotta cheese
finely grated rind of 1 lemon
90ml/6 tbsp dark (bittersweet)
  chocolate chips
75ml/5 tbsp chopped mixed peel
45ml/3 tbsp chopped angelica
For the chocolate and sherry pastry
225g/8oz/2 cups plain
  (all-purpose) flour
30ml/2 tbsp cocoa powder
  (unsweetened)
60ml/4 tbsp caster (superfine) sugar
115g/4oz/½ cup butter, diced
60ml/4 tbsp dry sherry

**1** Preheat the oven to 200°C/400°F/ Gas 6. To make the pastry, sift the flour and cocoa into a bowl, then stir in the sugar. Rub or cut in the butter until the mixture resembles fine breadcrumbs, then work in the dry sherry, using your fingertips, until the mixture binds to a firm, smooth dough.

**2** Roll out three-quarters of the pastry on a lightly floured surface and use to line a 24cm/9½in loose-based flan tin (quiche pan). Chill for 20 minutes.

**COOK'S TIP**
This chocolate tart is best served at room temperature, so if made in advance, chill it when cool, then, when needed, bring to room temperature before serving.

**3** Beat the egg yolks and sugar in a bowl, then add the ricotta cheese. Beat with a wooden spoon to mix thoroughly. Stir in the lemon rind, chocolate chips, mixed peel and angelica. Scrape the ricotta mixture into the pastry case and level the surface.

**4** Roll out the remaining pastry thinly and cut into narrow strips, then arrange these in a lattice over the filling. Bake for 15 minutes, then lower the oven temperature to 180°C/350°F/Gas 4 and bake for 30–35 minutes more until golden brown. Leave to cool in the tin.

# KEY LIME PIE

*THIS PIE IS ONE OF AMERICA'S FAVOURITES. AS THE NAME SUGGESTS, IT ORIGINATED IN THE FLORIDA KEYS, BUT IS NOW HUGELY POPULAR ALL OVER THE WORLD.*

SERVES TEN

INGREDIENTS

4 eggs, separated
400g/14oz can skimmed, sweetened
  condensed milk
grated rind and juice of 3 limes
a few drops of green food
  colouring (optional)
30ml/2 tbsp caster (superfine) sugar
300ml/½ pint/1¼ cups double
  (heavy) cream
2–3 limes, thinly sliced
thinly pared lime rind and fresh mint
  sprigs, to decorate
For the rich shortcrust pastry
225g/8oz/2 cups plain
  (all-purpose) flour
115g/4oz/½ cup chilled butter, diced
30ml/2 tbsp caster (superfine) sugar
2 egg yolks
pinch of salt
30ml/2 tbsp chilled water

**3** Preheat the oven to 200°C/400°F/ Gas 6. Trim off the excess pastry from around the edge of the pastry case using a sharp knife, then line the pastry case with baking parchment and fill with baking beans.

**4** Bake the pastry case for 10 minutes. Remove the parchment and beans and return the pastry case to the oven for 10 minutes more to lightly brown.

**6** Whisk the egg whites in a grease-free bowl until stiff peaks form. Whisk in the sugar, then fold into the lime mixture.

**7** Reduce the oven temperature to 160°C/325°F/Gas 3. Pour the lime filling into the pastry case. Bake for about 20 minutes, or until the pie has set and is starting to brown. Cool, then chill.

**1** To make the pastry, sift the flour into a large mixing bowl and rub or cut in the butter until the mixture resembles fine breadcrumbs. Add the sugar, egg yolks, salt and enough water to bind together. Knead lightly and briefly to form a soft dough.

**2** Roll out the pastry thinly on a lightly floured surface and use to line a deep 21cm/8½in fluted flan tin (quiche pan), allowing the excess pastry to hang over the edge. Prick the base of the pastry case all over with a fork, wrap in clear film (plastic wrap) and chill for at least 30 minutes.

**5** Meanwhile, beat the egg yolks in a large bowl until light and creamy, then beat in the condensed milk, along with the lime rind and juice. Add the food colouring, if using, and continue to beat until the mixture is thick.

**COOK'S TIP**
If short of time, you can make the pastry in a food processor, but take care not to overprocess it. Use the pulse button and process for a few seconds at a time; switch off the motor the moment the dough begins to clump together. Remove and knead lightly, then wrap and chill.

**8** Just before serving, whip the cream for the topping and spoon it around the edge of the pie. Cut the lime slices once from the centre to the edge, then twist each slice and arrange. Decorate with lime rind and sprigs of fresh mint.

# LEMON MERINGUE PIE

*CRISP SHORTCRUST IS FILLED WITH A MOUTHWATERING LEMON CREAM FILLING AND HEAPED WITH
SOFT GOLDEN-TOPPED MERINGUE. THIS CLASSIC DESSERT NEVER FAILS TO PLEASE.*

## SERVES SIX

INGREDIENTS
  3 large eggs, separated
  150g/5oz/⅔ cup caster
    (superfine) sugar
  grated rind and juice of 1 lemon
  25g/1oz/½ cup fresh
    white breadcrumbs
  250ml/8fl oz/1 cup milk
For the shortcrust pastry
  115g/4oz/1 cup plain
    (all-purpose) flour
  pinch of salt
  50g/2oz/¼ cup butter, diced
  50g/2oz/¼ cup lard or white
    vegetable fat, diced
  15ml/1 tbsp caster
    (superfine) sugar
  15ml/1 tbsp chilled water

**1** To make the pastry, sift the flour and salt into a mixing bowl. Rub or cut in the fats until the mixture resembles fine breadcrumbs. Stir in the caster sugar and enough chilled water to make a soft dough. Roll it out on a lightly floured surface and use to line a 21cm/8½in pie plate. Chill until required.

**2** Meanwhile, place the egg yolks and 30ml/2 tbsp of the caster sugar in a bowl. Add the lemon rind and juice, the breadcrumbs and milk, mix lightly and leave to soak for 1 hour.

**3** Preheat the oven to 200°C/400°F/Gas 6. Beat the filling until smooth and pour into the chilled pastry case. Bake for 20 minutes, or until the filling has just set. Remove the pie from the oven and cool on a wire rack for 30 minutes or until a slight skin has formed on the surface. Lower the oven temperature to 180°C/350°F/Gas 4.

**4** Whisk the egg whites until stiff peaks form. Gradually whisk in the remaining caster sugar to form a glossy meringue. Spoon on top of the lemon filling and spread right to the edge of the pastry, using the back of a spoon. Swirl the meringue slightly.

**5** Bake the pie for 20–25 minutes, or until the meringue is crisp and golden brown. Allow to cool on a wire rack for 10 minutes before serving.

# MISSISSIPPI MUD PIE

*THIS IS THE ULTIMATE IN CHOCOLATE DESSERTS – A DEEP PASTRY CASE, FILLED WITH CHOCOLATE CUSTARD AND TOPPED WITH A FLUFFY RUM MOUSSE AND A SMOTHERING OF WHIPPED CREAM.*

SERVES SIX TO EIGHT

INGREDIENTS
  3 eggs, separated
  20ml/4 tsp cornflour (cornstarch)
  75g/3oz/6 tbsp caster
    (superfine) sugar
  400ml/14fl oz/1¾ cups milk
  150g/5oz plain (semisweet)
    chocolate, broken up
  5ml/1 tsp vanilla essence (extract)
  15ml/1 tbsp powdered gelatine
  45ml/3 tbsp water
  30ml/2 tsp dark rum
  175g/6fl oz/¾ cup double (heavy)
    cream, whipped
  a few chocolate curls,
    to decorate
For the rich shortcrust pastry
  250g/9oz/2¼ cups plain
    (all-purpose) flour
  150g/5oz/⅔ cup butter, diced
  2 egg yolks
  15–30ml/1–2 tbsp chilled water

**1** To make the pastry, sift the flour into a bowl and rub or cut in the butter until the mixture resembles breadcrumbs. Stir in the egg yolks with just enough chilled water to make a soft dough.

**2** Roll out on a lightly floured surface and use to line a deep 23cm/9in flan tin (quiche pan). Chill for 30 minutes. Preheat the oven to 190°C/375°F/Gas 5. Prick the pastry all over with a fork, line with foil and baking beans, then bake blind for 10 minutes.

**3** Remove the foil and beans, return the pie to the oven and bake for about 10 minutes more until the pastry is crisp and golden. Cool in the tin.

**4** To make the custard filling, mix the egg yolks, cornflour and 30ml/2 tbsp of the sugar in a bowl. Heat the milk in a pan until almost boiling, then beat into the egg mixture.

**5** Return the custard mixture to the cleaned pan and stir over a low heat until the custard has thickened and is smooth. Pour half the custard into a bowl.

**6** Melt the chocolate in a heatproof bowl set over a pan of hot water, then add to the custard in the bowl. Add the vanilla essence and mix well. Spread in the pastry case, cover closely with some baking parchment to prevent a skin from forming, cool, then chill until set.

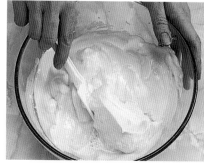

**7** Sprinkle the gelatine over the water in a small bowl, leave until spongy, then place over a pan of simmering water until all the gelatine has dissolved. Stir into the remaining custard, along with the rum. Whisk the egg whites until stiff peaks form, whisk in the remaining sugar, then quickly fold into the custard before it sets.

**8** Spoon the mixture over the chocolate custard to cover completely. Chill until set, then remove the pie from the tin to serve. Spread whipped cream over the top and decorate with chocolate curls.

# RICH PASTRY DESSERTS

*Not all sweet pies and pastries are filled with fruit. For pure indulgence, velvety smooth Coffee Custard Tart is unbeatable. You'll find it here alongside decadent chocolate desserts such as Dark Chocolate and Hazelnut Tart, a creamy Baked Cheesecake with Kissel and exotic desserts such as Moroccan Serpent Cake and that most classic of French pastries, Lemon Tart.*

# LEMON TART

*THIS CLASSIC FRENCH TART IS ONE OF THE MOST DELICIOUS DESSERTS THERE IS. A RICH LEMON CURD IS ENCASED IN A CRISP PASTRY CASE. CRÈME FRAÎCHE IS AN OPTIONAL — BUT NICE — EXTRA.*

SERVES SIX

6 eggs, beaten
350g/12oz/1½ cups caster
  (superfine) sugar
115g/4oz/½ cup butter
grated rind and juice of 4 lemons
icing (confectioners') sugar
  for dusting
For the pâte sucrée
225g/8oz/2 cups plain
  (all-purpose) flour
115g/4oz/½ cup butter, diced
30ml/2 tbsp icing
  (confectioners') sugar
1 egg
5ml/1 tsp vanilla
  essence (extract)
15ml/1 tbsp chilled water

**1** Preheat the oven to 200°C/400°F/ Gas 6. To make the pastry, sift the flour into a mixing bowl and rub or cut in the butter until the mixture resembles fine breadcrumbs. Stir in the icing sugar.

**2** Add the egg, vanilla essence and most of the chilled water, then work to a soft dough. Add a few more drops of water if necessary. Knead quickly and lightly until smooth.

**3** Roll out the pastry on a floured surface and use to line a 23cm/9in flan tin (quiche pan). Prick the base all over with a fork. Line with baking parchment and fill with baking beans. Bake the pastry case for 10 minutes. Remove the paper and beans and set the pastry case aside while you make the filling.

**4** Put the eggs, sugar and butter into a pan, and stir over a low heat until all the sugar has dissolved. Add the lemon rind and juice, and continue cooking, stirring constantly, until the lemon curd has thickened slightly.

**5** Pour the curd mixture into the pastry case. Bake for about 20 minutes, or until the lemon curd filling is just set. Transfer the tart to a wire rack to cool. Dust the surface of the tart generously with icing sugar just before serving.

# BUTTERNUT SQUASH AND MAPLE PIE

*THIS AMERICAN-STYLE PIE HAS A RICH SHORTCRUST PASTRY CASE AND A CREAMY FILLING, SWEETENED WITH MAPLE SYRUP AND FLAVOURED WITH FRESH GINGER AND A DASH OF BRANDY.*

SERVES TEN

INGREDIENTS
  1 small butternut squash
  60ml/4 tbsp water
  2.5cm/1in piece of fresh root ginger,
    peeled and grated
  120ml/4fl oz/½ cup double
    (heavy) cream
  90ml/6 tbsp maple syrup
  45ml/3 tbsp light muscovado
    (molasses) sugar
  3 eggs, lightly beaten
  30ml/2 tbsp brandy
  1.5ml/¼ tsp grated nutmeg
  beaten egg, to glaze
For the rich shortcrust pastry
  175g/6oz/1½ cups plain
    (all-purpose) flour
  pinch of salt
  115g/4oz/½ cup butter, diced
  10ml/2 tsp caster (superfine) sugar
  1 egg, lightly beaten

**1** To make the pastry, sift the flour and salt into a mixing bowl. Rub or cut in the butter until the mixture resembles fine breadcrumbs. Add the sugar and the egg. Mix to a dough. Wrap in clear film (plastic wrap). Chill for 30 minutes.

**2** Halve the butternut squash, peel and scoop out the seeds. Cut the flesh into cubes and put in a pan with the water. Cover and cook gently for 15 minutes. Remove the lid, stir in the ginger and cook for a further 5 minutes until all the liquid has evaporated and the squash is tender. Cool slightly, then purée in a food processor until smooth.

**3** Roll out the pastry and use to line a 23cm/9in flan tin (quiche pan). Gather up the trimmings, re-roll them thinly, then cut them into maple leaf shapes. Brush the edge of the pastry case with beaten egg and attach the maple leaf shapes at regular intervals to make a decorative rim. Cover with clear film and chill for 30 minutes.

**4** Put a heavy baking sheet in the oven and preheat to 200°C/400°F/Gas 6. Prick the pastry base with a fork and line with foil and fill with baking beans. Bake blind on the hot baking sheet for 12 minutes.

**5** Remove the foil and beans and bake for a further 5 minutes. Brush the base of the pastry case with beaten egg and return to the oven for about 3 minutes. Lower the oven temperature to 180°C/350°F/Gas 4.

**6** Mix 200g/7oz/scant 1 cup of the butternut purée with the cream, syrup, sugar, eggs, brandy and grated nutmeg. (Discard any remaining purée.) Pour into the pastry case. Bake for about 30 minutes, or until the filling is lightly set. Cool slightly, then serve with cream.

# DARK CHOCOLATE AND HAZELNUT TART

*THIS CRISP, HAZELNUT-FLAVOURED PASTRY TASTES WONDERFUL WITH A RICH CHOCOLATE FILLING.*

SERVES TEN

INGREDIENTS
    300ml/½ pint/1¼ cups double
      (heavy) cream
    150ml/¼ pint/⅔ cup creamy milk
    150g/5oz dark (bittersweet)
      chocolate, chopped
    4 eggs
    50g/2oz/¼ cup caster (superfine) sugar
    5ml/1 tsp vanilla essence (extract)
    15ml/1 tbsp plain (all-purpose) flour
    115g/4oz/1 cup toasted hazelnuts
    10ml/2 tsp icing
      (confectioners') sugar
For the hazelnut pastry
    150g/5oz/1¼ cups plain
      (all-purpose) flour
    pinch of salt
    45ml/3 tbsp caster (superfine) sugar
    50g/2oz/½ cup ground
      hazelnuts, toasted
    90g/3½oz/scant ½ cup butter, diced
    1 egg, lightly beaten

**1** To make the pastry, sift the flour, salt and sugar into a mixing bowl, then mix in the toasted hazelnuts. Rub or cut in the butter until the mixture resembles fine breadcrumbs.

**2** Make a well in the centre, add the beaten egg and mix to a firm dough. Knead the dough on a lightly floured surface for a few seconds until smooth. Wrap in clear film (plastic wrap) and chill for 30 minutes.

**3** Roll out the pastry on a floured surface and use to line a 23cm/9in loose-based heart-shaped flan tin (quiche pan). Trim the edges. Cover and chill for a further 30 minutes.

**4** Re-roll the pastry trimmings into a long strip, about 30cm/12in long. Cut this into six strips, each 5mm/¼in wide, and make two plaits (braids) with three pastry strips in each. Curve into a heart shape and press gently to join together at both ends. Carefully place the heart on a baking sheet lined with baking parchment and chill.

**5** Put a heavy baking sheet in the oven and preheat to 200°C/400°F/Gas 6. Prick the base of the pastry case with a fork. Line with foil and baking beans and bake blind for 10 minutes. Remove the foil and beans and bake for a further 5 minutes. Bake the pastry plait on the shelf below for 10 minutes, or until lightly browned.

**6** Pour the cream and milk into a pan and bring to the boil. Add the chocolate and stir until melted. Whisk the eggs, caster sugar, vanilla and flour together. Pour the hot chocolate cream over the egg mixture, whisking all the time. Stir in the chopped hazelnuts.

**7** Pour the chocolate and hazelnut mixture into the pastry case and bake for 25 minutes, or until just set. Allow to cool, then remove from the tin and transfer to a serving plate. Place the pastry rope on top, then lightly dust with icing sugar.

# CHOCOLATE, PEAR AND PECAN PIE

*A CLASSIC PIE GETS A TEMPTING NEW TASTE WITH DARK CHOCOLATE AND JUICY PEARS.*

SERVES EIGHT TO TEN

INGREDIENTS

   3 small pears, peeled
   165g/5½oz/scant ¾ cup caster
    (superfine) sugar
   150ml/¼ pint/⅔ cup water
   pared rind of 1 lemon
   50g/2oz plain (semisweet) chocolate,
    broken into pieces
   50g/2oz/¼ cup butter, diced
   225g/8oz/scant ¾ cup golden
    (light corn) syrup
   3 eggs, beaten
   5ml/1 tsp vanilla essence (extract)
   150g/5oz/1¼ cups pecan
    nuts, chopped
For the rich shortcrust pastry
   175g/6oz/½ cup plain
    (all-purpose) flour
   115g/4oz/½ cup butter, diced
   25g/1oz/2 tbsp caster
    (superfine) sugar
   1 egg yolk
   10–15ml/2–3 tsp chilled water

**1** To make the pastry, sift the flour into a mixing bowl and rub or cut in the butter. Stir in the sugar. Mix the egg yolk with 10ml/2 tsp of the water, add to the dry ingredients and mix to a dough, adding more water if necessary. Knead for a few seconds until smooth. Wrap the dough in clear film (plastic wrap) and chill for 30 minutes.

**2** Preheat the oven to 200°F/400°C/ Gas 6. Roll out the pastry and line a deep 23cm/9in fluted flan tin (quiche pan). Chill the case for 20 minutes, then line it with foil and baking beans. Bake for 10 minutes. Lift out the foil and beans and bake for 5 minutes more. Set aside to cool.

**3** Cut the pears in half and remove the cores with a small spoon. Place 50g/ 2oz/¼ cup of the sugar in a pan with the water. Add the lemon rind and bring to the boil. Add the pears. Cover, lower the heat and simmer for 10 minutes. Remove the pears from the pan and set aside to cool. Discard the liquid.

**4** Place the chocolate into a heatproof bowl and melt over a pan of simmering water. Beat in the butter, then set aside. In a separate pan, heat the remaining sugar and syrup together until most of the sugar has dissolved. Bring to the boil and simmer for 2 minutes.

**5** Whisk the eggs into the chocolate mixture until combined, then whisk in the syrup mixture. Stir in the vanilla essence and pecan nuts.

**6** Place the pear halves flat side down on a board. Using a fine sharp knife, make lengthways cuts all along each pear, taking care not to cut all the way through. Using a palette knife (metal spatula), lift the pears into the pastry case and arrange. Pour the pecan mixture over the top, so that the pears are still visible through the mixture.

**7** Bake for 25–30 minutes, or until the filling is set, then leave to cool on a wire rack before removing the pie from the tin and serving, in slices.

# WALNUT PIE

*SWEETENED WITH COFFEE-FLAVOURED MAPLE SYRUP, THIS PIE HAS A RICH AND STICKY TEXTURE.
THE WALNUTS CAN BE REPLACED BY PECAN NUTS FOR AN AUTHENTIC AMERICAN PIE.*

**SERVES EIGHT**

INGREDIENTS
  30ml/2 tbsp ground coffee
  175ml/6fl oz/¾ cup maple syrup
  25g/1oz/2 tbsp butter, softened
  175g/6oz/¾ cup soft light
    brown sugar
  3 eggs, beaten
  5ml/1 tsp vanilla essence (extract)
  115g/4oz/1 cup walnut halves
For the pâte sucrée
  150g/5oz/1¼ cups plain
    (all-purpose) flour
  pinch of salt
  25g/1oz/¼ cup icing
    (confectioners') sugar
  75g/3oz/6 tbsp butter, diced
  2 egg yolks

**2** Knead the pastry on a lightly floured surface for a few seconds until smooth. Wrap in clear film (plastic wrap) and chill for 30 minutes.

**3** Roll out the pastry and use to line a 20cm/8in fluted flan tin (quiche pan). Line with baking parchment and baking beans and bake for about 10 minutes. Remove the paper and beans and bake for a further 5 minutes until brown. Set the pastry case aside. Lower the oven temperature to 180°C/350°F/Gas 4.

**4** Heat the coffee and maple syrup in a pan until almost boiling. Set aside to cool slightly. Mix the butter and sugar in a bowl, then gradually beat in the eggs. Strain the reserved maple syrup mixture into the bowl, add the vanilla essence and stir well.

**1** Preheat the oven to 200°C/400°F/ Gas 6. To make the pastry, sift the flour, salt and icing sugar into a mixing bowl. Rub or cut in the butter until the mixture resembles fine breadcrumbs. Add the egg yolks and mix well to form a soft dough.

**5** Arrange the walnuts in the pastry case, then carefully pour in the filling. Bake for 30–35 minutes, or until lightly browned and firm. Allow to cool for a few minutes before serving warm with crème fraîche or vanilla ice cream.

# ALMOND AND PINE NUT TART

*STRANGE THOUGH IT MAY SEEM, THIS TRADITIONAL TART IS AN ITALIAN VERSION OF THE HOMELY BAKEWELL TART FROM DERBYSHIRE IN ENGLAND.*

SERVES EIGHT

INGREDIENTS
  115g/4oz/½ cup butter, softened
  115g/4oz/½ cup caster
    (superfine) sugar
  1 egg, plus 2 egg yolks
  150g/5oz/1¼ cups ground almonds
  115g/4oz/1⅓ cups pine nuts
  60ml/4 tbsp seedless raspberry jam
  icing (confectioners') sugar,
    for dusting
For the rich shortcrust pastry
  175g/6oz/1½ cups plain
    (all-purpose) flour
  65g/2½oz/⅓ cup caster
    (superfine) sugar
  1.5ml/¼ tsp baking powder
  pinch of salt
  115g/4oz/½ cup chilled butter, diced
  1 egg yolk

**1** To make the pastry, sift the flour, sugar, baking powder and salt on to a clean, dry cold surface or marble pastry board. Make a well in the centre and put in the diced butter and egg yolk. Gradually work the flour mixture into the butter and egg yolk, using just your fingertips, until you have a soft, pliable dough.

**2** Press the dough into a 23cm/9in loose-based fluted flan tin (quiche pan). Chill for 30 minutes.

**3** Cream the butter and sugar with an electric mixer until light, then use a wooden spoon to beat in the egg and egg yolks a little at a time, alternating them with the almonds. Beat in the nuts.

**4** Preheat the oven to 160°C/325°F/Gas 3. Spread the jam evenly over the pastry base, then spoon in the filling. Bake for 30–35 minutes until golden, or until a skewer inserted in the centre of the tart comes out clean.

**5** Transfer to a wire rack and leave to cool, then carefully remove the side of the tin, leaving the tart on the tin base. Dust with icing sugar and serve with whipped cream.

**COOK'S TIP**
This pastry is too sticky to roll out, so simply mould it into the base and sides of the tin with your fingers.

# COFFEE CUSTARD TART

*FOR SHEER DECADENCE, TRY THIS CRISP WALNUT PASTRY CASE, FLAVOURED WITH VANILLA AND FILLED WITH A SMOOTH CREAMY COFFEE CUSTARD. IT IS BAKED UNTIL LIGHTLY SET AND TOPPED WITH CREAM.*

SERVES SIX TO EIGHT

INGREDIENTS
  1 vanilla pod (bean)
  30ml/2 tbsp ground coffee
  300ml/½ pint/1¼ cups single
    (light) cream
  150ml/¼ pint/⅔ cup milk
  2 eggs, plus 2 egg yolks
  50g/2oz/¼ cup caster
    (superfine) sugar
  icing (confectioners') sugar,
    for dusting
  whipped cream, to serve
For the walnut pastry
  175g/6oz/1½ cups plain
    (all-purpose) flour
  30ml/2 tbsp icing
    (confectioners') sugar
  115g/4oz/½ cup butter, diced
  75g/3oz/¾ cup walnuts, chopped
  1 egg yolk
  5ml/1 tsp vanilla essence (extract)
  10ml/2 tsp chilled water

**1**  To make the pastry, sift the flour and sugar into a mixing bowl. Rub or cut in the butter until the mixture resembles fine breadcrumbs. Stir in the walnuts.

**2**  In a small bowl, mix together the egg yolk, vanilla and water. Add to the dry ingredients and mix to a smooth dough. Wrap in clear film (plastic wrap) and chill for about 20 minutes. Put a heavy baking sheet in the oven and preheat to 200°C/400°F/Gas 6.

**3**  Roll out the pastry and use to line a 20cm/8in flan tin (quiche pan) or flan ring, using a knife to trim the edges. Chill again for 20 minutes.

**4**  Prick the base all over with a fork. Fill the pastry case with foil and baking beans and bake on the baking sheet for 10 minutes. Remove the foil and beans, and bake the case for 10 minutes more. Reduce the oven temperature to 150°C/300°F/Gas 2.

**5**  Meanwhile, split the vanilla pod and scrape out the seeds. Put both in a pan with the coffee, cream and milk. Heat until almost boiling, remove from the heat, cover and infuse for 10 minutes. Whisk the eggs, egg yolks and caster sugar together in a bowl.

**6**  Return the cream mixture to the heat, bring to the boil, then pour on to the egg mixture, stirring constantly. Strain into the pastry case. Bake for 40–45 minutes, or until lightly set. Cool on a wire rack. Serve dusted with icing sugar and topped with whirls of cream.

# PEAR TARTE TATIN <u>WITH</u> CARDAMOM

*CARDAMOM IS A SPICE THAT IS EQUALLY AT HOME IN SWEET AND SAVOURY DISHES. IT IS DELICIOUS WITH PEARS, AND BRINGS OUT THEIR FLAVOUR BEAUTIFULLY IN THIS SIMPLE TART.*

SERVES FOUR TO SIX

INGREDIENTS
   50g/2oz/¼ cup butter, softened
   50g/2oz/¼ cup caster
   (superfine) sugar
   seeds from 10 green
   cardamom pods
   225g/8oz puff pastry
   3 ripe, large round pears

**1** Preheat the oven to 220°C/425°F/ Gas 7. Spread the butter over the base of a 18cm/7in heavy ovenproof omelette pan. Sprinkle with the sugar, then sprinkle the cardamom seeds over.

**2** On a lightly floured work surface, roll out the pastry to a circle slightly larger than the pan. Prick the pastry all over with a fork, place on a baking sheet and chill.

**3** Peel the pears, cut in half lengthways and remove the cores. Arrange the pears, rounded side down, in the pan. Heat until the sugar melts and begins to bubble with the juice from the pears.

**4** Once the sugar has caramelized remove the pan from the heat. Place the pastry on top, tucking in the edges with a knife. Bake for 25 minutes.

**5** Leave the tart in the pan for about 2 minutes until the juices have stopped bubbling. Invert a serving plate over the pan then, wearing oven gloves to protect your hands, hold the pan and plate together and quickly turn over, gently shaking it to release the tart. It may be necessary to slide a spatula underneath the pears to loosen them. Serve the tart warm, with cream.

# BAKED CHEESECAKE WITH KISSEL

*AS WITH ALL CLASSIC CHEESECAKES, THIS SIMPLE GERMAN VERSION IS BAKED IN A RICH SHORTCRUST PASTRY CASE, FLAVOURED HERE WITH LEMON. KISSEL IS A TRADITIONAL RED BERRY COMPÔTE.*

SERVES EIGHT TO TEN

INGREDIENTS
675g/1½lb/3 cups quark or low-fat
    soft white cheese
4 eggs, separated
150g/5oz/⅔ cup caster
    (superfine) sugar
45ml/3 tbsp cornflour (cornstarch)
150ml/¼ pint/⅔ cup sour cream
finely grated rind and juice of
    ½ lemon
5ml/1 tsp vanilla essence (extract)
fresh mint sprigs, to decorate
For the rich shortcrust pastry
225g/8oz/2 cups plain
    (all-purpose) flour
115g/4oz/½ cup butter, diced
15ml/1 tbsp caster (superfine) sugar
finely grated rind of ½ lemon
1 egg, beaten
For the kissel
450g/1lb/4–4½ cups prepared red
    berry fruit
50g/2oz/¼ cup caster
    (superfine) sugar
120ml/4fl oz/½ cup water
15ml/1 tbsp arrowroot

**1** To make the pastry, sift the flour into a large mixing bowl. Rub or cut in the butter until the mixture resembles fine breadcrumbs. Stir in the sugar and lemon rind, then add the beaten egg and mix to a dough. Wrap in clear film (plastic wrap) and chill for 30 minutes.

**2** Roll out the pastry and use to line a 25cm/10in loose-based fluted flan tin (quiche pan). Chill for 1 hour.

**3** Place the quark or soft white cheese in a fine sieve set over a bowl and leave to drain for 1 hour.

**4** Preheat the oven to 200°C/400°F/ Gas 6. Prick the base of the chilled pastry case all over with a fork, fill it with crumpled foil and bake for about 5 minutes. Remove the foil and bake for a further 5 minutes. Remove the pastry case from the oven and lower the oven temperature to 180°C/350°F/Gas 4.

**5** Put the drained quark or soft cheese in a bowl with the egg yolks and caster sugar and mix together.

**6** Blend the cornflour in a cup with a little of the sour cream, then add to the cheese mixture along with the remaining sour cream, the lemon rind and juice and vanilla essence. Mix thoroughly with a wooden spoon.

**7** Whisk the egg whites in a grease-free bowl until stiff, then fold into the cheese mixture, one-third at a time. Pour the filling into the pastry case and bake for 1–1¼ hours, or until golden and firm. Switch off the oven and leave the door slightly ajar. Let the cheesecake cool down in the oven, then remove it and chill for 2 hours.

**8** To make the kissel, put the prepared fruit, caster sugar and water into a pan and cook over a low heat until the sugar dissolves and the juices begin to run. Remove the fruit with a slotted spoon and put in a bowl. Set aside. Retain the fruit juices in the pan.

**9** Mix the arrowroot with a little cold water in a cup. Stir the mixture into the reserved fruit juices in the pan and bring to the boil, stirring constantly. Return the fruit to the pan, mix well, then allow to cool.

**10** Serve the well-chilled cheesecake in slices, spooning a little of the kissel over each portion. Decorate with sprigs of mint and fresh berries.

# PEACH AND BRANDY PIE

*SLICES OF JUICY, RIPE PEACHES, GENTLY COOKED IN BUTTER AND SUGAR, ARE ENCASED IN CRISP PUFF PASTRY TO MAKE THIS FRAGRANT FRUIT PIE — SIMPLE BUT DELICIOUS.*

**5** Preheat the oven to 200°C/400°F/ Gas 6. Remove the clear film from the pastry rounds. Spoon the peaches into the middle of the larger round and use a spoon to spread them out to within about 2cm/2in of the edge.

**6** Place the smaller pastry round on top, shaping it in a mound over the peaches. Brush the edge of the larger pastry round with water, then fold this over the top pastry round and press to seal. Twist the edges together to make a pattern all the way round.

**7** Make the glaze by mixing the egg and water together in a cup. Lightly brush it over the pastry and sprinkle over the granulated sugar, spreading it evenly over the pastry. Make five or six small crescent-shape slashes on the top of the pastry, radiating from the centre towards the edge.

**8** Bake the pie for about 45 minutes, or until the pastry is risen and golden brown. Serve warm in slices with vanilla ice cream.

SERVES EIGHT

INGREDIENTS
    6 large, firm ripe peaches
    40g/1½oz/3 tbsp butter
    45ml/3 tbsp brandy
    75g/3oz/6 tbsp caster
      (superfine) sugar
    450g/1lb puff pastry
    vanilla ice cream, to serve
For the glaze
    1 egg
    5ml/1 tsp water
    15ml/1 tbsp granulated sugar

**1** Immerse the peaches in boiling water for about 30 seconds. Lift them out with a slotted spoon, dip in cold water, then peel off the skins. Halve and stone (pit) the peaches, then cut into slices.

**2** Melt the butter in a large frying pan. Add the peach slices, then sprinkle with the brandy and sugar. Cook for about 4 minutes, shaking the pan frequently, or until the sugar has dissolved and the peaches are tender. Set the pan aside to cool.

**3** Cut the pastry into two pieces, one very slightly larger than the other. Roll out on a lightly floured surface and, using plates or cake tins as a guide, cut the larger piece of pastry into a 30cm/ 12in circle and the smaller one into a 28cm/11in circle.

**4** Place the pastry rounds on separate large baking sheets lined with baking parchment, cover with clear film (plastic wrap) and chill for 30 minutes.

# STRAWBERRY TART

*THIS TART IS BEST ASSEMBLED JUST BEFORE SERVING, BUT YOU CAN BAKE THE PASTRY CASE EARLY IN THE DAY. MAKE THE FILLING AHEAD OF TIME AND PUT IT TOGETHER IN A FEW MINUTES.*

### SERVES SIX

INGREDIENTS
  350g/12oz rough puff or puff pastry
  225g/8oz/1 cup cream cheese
  grated rind of ½ orange
  30ml/2 tbsp orange liqueur or
    orange juice
  45–60ml/3–4 tbsp icing
    (confectioners') sugar, plus extra for
    dusting (optional)
  450g/1lb/4 cups strawberries, hulled

**1** Roll out the pastry on a lightly floured surface to a thickness of about 3mm/⅛in and use to line a 28 × 10cm/ 11 × 4in tranche tin. Trim the edges of the pastry neatly with a knife, then chill for 30 minutes. Preheat the oven to 200°C/400°F/Gas 6.

**2** Prick the base of the pastry all over. Line the pastry case with foil, fill with baking beans and bake for 15 minutes. Remove the foil and beans and bake for 10 minutes more until the pastry is browned. Gently press down on the pastry base to deflate it, then leave to cool on a wire rack.

**3** Using a hand-held electric whisk or food processor, beat together well the cream cheese, orange rind, liqueur or orange juice and icing sugar. Spread the cheese filling in the pastry case. Halve the strawberries and arrange them on top of the cheese filling. Dust with icing sugar, if you like.

# GÂTEAU SAINT-HONORÉ

*NAMED AFTER THE PATRON SAINT OF BAKERS, THIS SPECTACULAR DESSERT HAS A PUFF PASTRY BASE TOPPED WITH CARAMEL-COATED CHOUX PUFFS AND FILLED WITH CRÈME PÂTISSIÈRE.*

SERVES TEN

INGREDIENTS
  175g/6oz puff pastry
For the choux pastry
  300ml/½ pint/1¼ cups water
  115g/4oz/½ cup butter, diced
  130g/4½oz/scant 1¼ cups plain
    (all-purpose) flour, sifted
  2.5ml/½ tsp salt
  4 eggs, lightly beaten
  beaten egg, to glaze
For the crème pâtissière
  3 egg yolks
  50g/2oz/¼ cup caster
    (superfine) sugar
  30ml/2 tbsp plain (all-purpose) flour
  30ml/2 tbsp cornflour (cornstarch)
  300ml/½ pint/1¼ cups milk
  150ml/¼ pint/⅔ cup double
    (heavy) cream
  30ml/2 tbsp orange liqueur, such as
    Grand Marnier
For the caramel
  225g/8oz/1 cup granulated sugar
  120ml/4fl oz/½ cup water

**1** Roll out the puff pastry on a lightly floured surface and cut out a 20cm/8in circle. Use a flan ring or an upturned plate as your guide. Place the pastry round on a baking sheet lined with baking parchment, prick all over with a fork and chill while you are making the choux pastry.

**2** To make the choux pastry, put the water and butter in a large pan. Heat until the butter has melted, then bring to the boil.

**3** Quickly tip in all the flour with the salt, remove the pan from the heat and beat vigorously until the mixture leaves the sides of the pan. Beat in the eggs, a little at a time, to form a paste.

**4** Preheat the oven to 200°C/400°F/ Gas 6. Spoon the choux pastry into a piping (pastry) bag fitted with a 1cm/ ½in plain nozzle. Pipe a spiral of choux on to the puff pastry base, starting at the edge and working to the centre.

**5** Use the remaining choux pastry to pipe 16 small buns on to a baking sheet lined with baking parchment. Brush the buns and the choux pastry spiral with egg to glaze. Bake the small buns for about 20 minutes and the choux-topped puff pastry on the shelf below for about 35 minutes, or until well risen.

**6** Pierce several holes in the top and sides of the spiral, and pierce one small hole in the side of each bun, using a fine skewer. Return the pastry to the oven for 5 minutes more to dry out. Cool on a wire rack.

**7** To make the crème pâtissière filling, whisk the egg yolks and caster sugar until light and creamy. Whisk in the flour and cornflour. Bring the milk to the boil in a pan and pour over the egg mixture, whisking all the time. Return the custard to the cleaned pan and cook for 2–3 minutes, until thickened and smooth. Cover with dampened baking parchment and leave to cool.

**8** Whip the cream lightly and fold in to the crème pâtissière with the orange liqueur. Spoon half into a piping bag fitted with a small plain nozzle and use to fill the choux buns.

**9** To make the caramel, heat the sugar and water in a pan until completely dissolved, stirring occasionally. Bring to the boil and cook until it turns a rich golden colour. Remove the pan from the heat and set over a large bowl half-filled with just boiled water to keep the caramel liquid.

**10** Place the puff and choux pastry base on a serving plate. Dip the bases of the choux buns, one at a time, into the caramel and arrange in a ring around the edge of the pastry case.

**11** Pipe the remaining crème pâtissière into the centre of the case. Drizzle the tops of the choux buns with the remaining caramel and leave to set. Set aside in a cool place for up to 2 hours before serving.

# APPLE STRUDEL

*THIS CLASSIC RECIPE IS USUALLY MADE WITH STRUDEL DOUGH, WHICH IS WONDERFUL, BUT CAN BE TRICKY AND TIME-CONSUMING, ESPECIALLY FOR A NOVICE. FILO PASTRY MAKES A GOOD SHORTCUT.*

SERVES EIGHT TO TEN

INGREDIENTS
  500g/1¼lb filo pastry, thawed
    if frozen
  115g/4oz/½ cup unsalted (sweet)
    butter, melted
  icing (confectioners') sugar,
    for dusting
For the filling
  1kg/2¼lb cooking apples, peeled,
    cored and sliced
  115g/4oz/2 cups fresh white
    breadcrumbs
  150g/5oz/¾ cup granulated sugar
  5ml/1 tsp cinnamon
  75g/3oz/generous ½ cup raisins
  finely grated rind of 1 lemon
  50g/2oz/¼ cup butter

**1** Preheat the oven to 180°C/350°F/ Gas 4. To make the filling, place the sliced apples in a large mixing bowl. Add the breadcrumbs, sugar, cinnamon, raisins and grated lemon rind and mix well. Melt the butter in a small pan, then stir it in to the mixture.

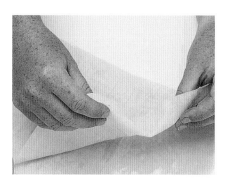

**2** Lay a sheet of filo pastry on a lightly floured work surface and brush with a little melted butter. Place another sheet on top and brush with melted butter as before. Continue stacking the sheets and brushing with the butter until there are four or five layers in all.

**3** Spoon the filling into the centre of the pastry, leaving a 2.5cm/1in border all round. Fold in the two shorter sides, then roll up from one long side, Swiss-roll (jelly-roll) style. Place the strudel on a lightly buttered baking sheet, seam side down. Brush the pastry with the remaining melted butter. Bake for 30–40 minutes, or until golden.

**4** Remove the strudel from the oven and place on a wire rack to cool. Dust with icing sugar before cutting into slices for serving.

**VARIATION**
For extra crunch in the strudel filling, add 75g/3oz/¾ cup lightly toasted, chopped hazelnuts or almonds.

# MOROCCAN SERPENT CAKE

*THIS IS PERHAPS THE MOST FAMOUS OF ALL MOROCCAN PASTRIES, FILLED WITH LIGHTLY FRAGRANT ALMOND PASTE, AND DUSTED WITH ICING SUGAR AND CINNAMON.*

SERVES EIGHT

INGREDIENTS
8 sheets of filo pastry, thawed
  if frozen
50g/2oz/¼ cup butter, melted
1 egg, beaten
5ml/1 tsp ground cinnamon
icing (confectioners') sugar,
  for dusting
For the almond paste
  about 50g/2oz/¼ cup butter, melted
  225g/8oz/2⅔ cups ground almonds
  2.5ml/½ tsp almond essence (extract)
  50g/2oz/½ cup icing
    (confectioners') sugar
  1 egg yolk, beaten
  15ml/1 tbsp rose water or orange
    flower water

**1** To make the almond paste, mix the melted butter with the ground almonds and almond essence in a bowl. Add the sugar, egg yolk and rose or orange flower water, mix well and knead until soft and pliable. Chill for 10 minutes.

**2** Break the paste into 10 even-size balls and, with your hands, roll them into 10cm/4in sausages. Chill again.

**3** Preheat the oven to 180°C/350°F/ Gas 4. Place two sheets of filo pastry on the work surface so that they overlap slightly to form an 18 × 56cm/7 × 22in rectangle. Brush the overlapping pastry edges to secure and then lightly brush all over with butter. Cover with another two sheets of filo in the same way and brush again with butter.

**4** Place five almond paste sausages along the lower edge of the filo sheet and roll up the pastry tightly, tucking in the ends. Repeat with the remaining filo and almond paste, so that you have two rolls. Brush a large baking sheet with butter. Shape the first roll into a loose coil, then transfer to the baking sheet. Attach the second roll and continue coiling the filo to make a snake. Tuck the end under.

**5** In a bowl, beat the egg with half the cinnamon. Brush over the pastry, then bake in the oven for 25 minutes until golden brown. Carefully invert the snake on to another baking sheet and return to the oven for 5–10 minutes more.

**6** Transfer the cake to a serving plate. Dust with icing sugar, then sprinkle with the remaining cinnamon. Serve warm.

# FILO-TOPPED APPLE PIE

*SCRUNCHED UP FILO PASTRY, BRUSHED WITH A LITTLE MELTED BUTTER IS THE VERY EASIEST WAY TO TOP A PIE. A LIGHT DUSTING OF ICING SUGAR GIVES IT AN ATTRACTIVE FINISH.*

SERVES SIX

INGREDIENTS
    900g/2lb cooking apples
    75g/3oz/6 tbsp caster
        (superfine) sugar
    grated rind of 1 lemon
    15ml/1 tbsp lemon juice
    75g/3oz/½ cup sultanas
        (golden raisins)
    2.5ml/½ tsp ground cinnamon
    4 large sheets of filo pastry, thawed
        if frozen
    25g/1oz/2 tbsp butter, melted
    icing (confectioners') sugar,
        for dusting

**VARIATION**
Any number of fruit fillings work well in this pie. A mixture of blackberries and apples is a good combination.

**1** Peel, core and dice the apples. Place them in a pan with the caster sugar and lemon rind. Drizzle the lemon juice over. Bring to the boil, stir well, then cook for 5 minutes or until the apples are soft. Stir in the sultanas and cinnamon. Pour the mixture into a 1.2 litre/2 pint/5 cup pie dish and level the top with a spoon. Leave to cool.

**2** Preheat the oven to 180°C/350°F/ Gas 4. Place a pie funnel in the centre of the fruit. Brush each sheet of filo with melted butter. Scrunch up loosely and place on the fruit to cover it.

**3** Bake for 20–30 minutes until the filo is golden. Dust the pie with icing sugar. Serve with custard, if you like.

# FRESH FIG FILO TART

*DESSERTS DON'T COME MUCH EASIER THAN THIS — FRESH FIGS IN CRISP FILO PASTRY, WITH A CREAMY ALMOND BATTER. THE TART TASTES WONDERFUL SERVED WITH CREAM OR YOGURT.*

SERVES SIX TO EIGHT

INGREDIENTS

5 sheets of filo pastry, each measuring 35 x 25cm/14 x 10in, thawed if frozen
25g/1oz/2 tbsp butter, melted
6 fresh figs, cut into wedges
75g/3oz/¾ cup plain (all-purpose) flour
75g/3oz/6 tbsp caster (superfine) sugar
4 eggs
450ml/¾ pint/scant 2 cups creamy milk
2.5ml/½ tsp almond essence (extract)
15ml/1 tbsp icing (confectioners') sugar, for dusting

**3** Sift the flour into a bowl and stir in the caster sugar. Add the eggs and a little of the milk and whisk until smooth. Gradually whisk in the remaining milk and the almond essence. Pour the batter over the figs.

**4** Bake for 1 hour or until the batter has set and is golden. Remove the tart from the oven and allow it to cool in the tin on a wire rack for 10 minutes. Dust with the icing sugar and serve with whipped cream or Greek yogurt.

**1** Preheat the oven to 190°C/375°F/Gas 5. Grease a 25 × 16cm/10 × 6¼in baking tin with butter. Brush each filo sheet in turn with melted butter and use to line the prepared tin.

**2** Trim the excess pastry, leaving a little overhanging the edge. Arrange the figs over the base of the tart.

# INDEX